The
Betta

An Owner's Guide To

A HAPPY HEALTHY FISH

Howell Book House

Howell Book House
An Imprint of Macmillan General Reference USA
A Pearson Education Macmillan Company
1633 Broadway
New York, NY 10019-6785

Library of Congress Cataloging-in-Publication Data
Hargrove, Mic.
The Betta: an owner's guide to a happy healthy fish / Mic and Maddy Hargrove.
     p.   cm.
Includes bibliographical references
ISBN 1-58245-050-1

1. Siamese fighting fish.   I. Hargrove, Maddy.   II. Title.
SF458.B4H27   1999
639.3'77—dc21   99-24777
                       CIP

Manufactured in the United States of America
10 9 8 7 6 5 4 3 2 1

Series Director: Amanda Pisani
Book Design: Michele Laseau
Cover Design: Iris Jeromnimon
Illustration: Steve Adams
Production Team: Diana Francoeur, David Faust, Faunette Johnston, Clint Lahnen,
  Dennis Sheehan, Terri Sheehan

Contents

All
About

part one

Bettas

External Features of the Betta

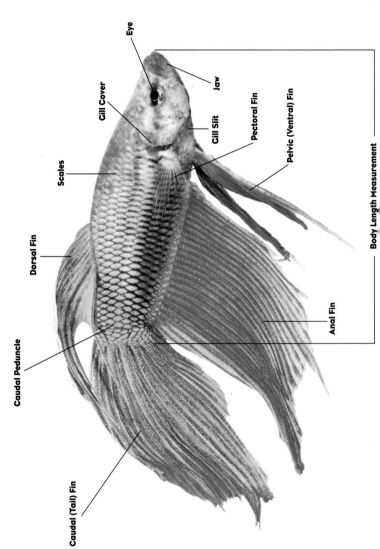

Eye

Jaw

Gill Cover

Gill Slit

Pectoral Fin

Scales

Pelvic (Ventral) Fin

Body Length Measurement

Dorsal Fin

Anal Fin

Caudal Peduncle

Caudal (Tail) Fin

chapter 1

The **Jewel** of the **Orient**

Welcome to the enchanting and amazing world of the betta, one of the most beautiful inhabitants of the tropical aquarium. Tropical fish keeping is fascinating, providing an underwater world that is diverse in color and style, one that will give you and your family years of never-ending enjoyment.

Tropical fish keeping is also a great challenge that offers the highest rewards of satisfaction, relaxation and pride that go hand in hand with the success that you will experience when you set up and maintain a healthy aquarium for your new betta.

5

The Betta's Realm

Imagine for a moment a cheerful and brightly colored aquarium. An airstone bubbles merrily in one corner as the wispy and delicate leaves of a green cabomba plant sway gently in the filter's current. As your eyes drift toward the center of the tank, you notice a bright red betta with majestic flowing fins moving casually along as it patiently surveys its surroundings. Beneath, a group of vividly colored platys displays the natural colors and warmth of the noonday sun. Sounds inviting doesn't it? This is the enchanting realm of the betta.

If you are as dedicated and delighted with the fascinating world of tropical fish as I am, then we share a common passion that has captured the interest and hearts of a wide variety of hobbyists for over a century. The betta has withstood this test of time, and has become a favorite choice among freshwater aquarium keepers for many years. So now, let our exploration into the amazing world of the betta begin.

Natural Habitat

In its homeland waters of Thailand, the betta is referred to by local workers as "the jewel of the Orient." It is in this region that bettas can be found living in shallow rice paddies, stagnant pools, polluted streams, and other types of areas in which the water has a low-oxygen content.

In these rice paddies, the air temperature can reach 90°F. Direct rays of sunlight striking the shallow water can force the temperature of the paddy to reach a similar level. In nature, bettas live in a climate that is hot and moist all year long, and so they generally do best in water that is 79° to 82°F, slightly warmer than the water temperature favored by other freshwater tropical fish, which prefer a temperature between 76° and 78°F.

A History of Betta Keeping

The betta *(Betta picta)* was first described in 1846 by Valenciennes and Cuvier. C. Regan gave this marvelous fish the scientific name *Betta splendens* after the first shipment arrived in the United States in 1909. The beautiful betta strains that can be found in today's tropical fish market can be easily traced to the Asians who have been developing this fish's vivid colors and elegant, long fins for more than a century. These brilliant new strains no longer resemble the plain-looking wild bettas from which they were originally developed. Americans such as Warren Young have also contributed much to the production and development of the long-finned and highly colorful bettas that you can buy today. Young developed the Libby betta, the prototype of the large variety of strains that are now available.

FUN AQUARIUM FACTS

1. Aquarium keeping is now the fastest-growing hobby.

2. Twelve million homes in the United States have aquariums.

3. The internet has over 1,000 tropical fish sites.

4. Twenty-five million homes in Europe have aquariums.

5. Tropical fish keeping can lower stress and help you to live longer.

Each year, because of commercial selective breeding, the hobbyist has even more choices among a wide variety of patterns and fin styles. Most tropical fish shops will have several of the 23 different betta species on hand to match almost any individual taste.

BETTA FIGHTING

In Thailand, the betta is known as *pla kat,* which means tearing or biting fish. Here, wild bettas are collected and then selectively crossed with more aggressive-natured domesticated species in order to create champion fighters. Two male bettas are often placed together in a suspended glass bowl where they fight as part of a spectator sport. Large monetary bets are placed on these tough competitors, who are much more aggressive than their domestic counterparts.

Despite the fact that the two bettas are usually not allowed to fight until death in these cruel competitions, the sad fact remains that many males die shortly afterward from injuries sustained during the bout. Fortunately, in the United States betta fighting is considered immoral, and is illegal. Forcing two male bettas to fight is an unfortunate tragedy and the ultimate example of human unkindness toward nature.

The Betta Family

Bettas belong to the group of labyrinth fishes *(Anabantids)* that are known for their physical ability to breathe air. Other members of this unique family include gouramis *(Trichogaster)*, paradise fishes *(Macropodus)* and the climbing perch *(Anabas testudineus)*, which can even use this air-breathing trait to move short distances across land.

Like the betta, the pearl gourami is a member of the labyrinth group of fishes.

Betta Behavior

There is quite a physical difference between the wild betta and the captive-bred fighting fish. The fighting fish is stockier and has a pug nose. The betta that is taken from its natural habitat is more sedate and rarely fights. In the wild, male bettas fight with each other only to defend their territories or mating partners, but these "showy" rituals are often limited to threatening displays of flared gills and spread fins. These confrontations rarely end in death. Usually, one male retreats in defeat and is left unharmed.

In the confinement of a home aquarium, a betta's aggressive behavior toward other males of the same species will be intensified because of the smaller habitat and the lack of escape routes. That is why only one male betta should be kept in an aquarium. A betta can make a great addition to many types of community aquariums, as long as there is only one male per tank.

Female bettas fight with each other on occasion, but this is a rare occurrence. Once in a while, a little fin nipping and other acts of bad temper take place among squabbling females, but usually there is little or no serious damage. In general, it is not advisable to place a male and a female betta together in a community aquarium, because it is possible that other innocent tankmates may be injured should the pair decide to bicker or spawn.

Don't keep two male bettas together, as they will viciously defend their territory in the tank. These two males are actually separated by a glass partition and did not injure one another.

Tankmates for the betta are generally not a problem as long as they are kept with other types of community fish that are not aggressive. Guppies, swordtails, platys and mollies make superb additions to a betta tank, unless you purchase one that happens to be an overly aggressive fish or has suddenly decided to become a fin-nipper. A betta can be chased to the point of exhaustion and collapse by any fish that decides to take a small taste of its beautiful fins.

Providing a Suitable Environment

Because of the betta's reputation for physical hardiness, many hobbyists over the years have provided their bettas with inadequate living accommodations (small glass bowls and jars) and poor water conditions. While it is true that a betta may be capable of living for several years (actually just surviving) in a small bowl of cool water, it will never reach its full coloration and high quality of life if it is continually kept in this unsatisfactory manner.

Bettas deserve the same good care and quality aquarium conditions that are normally provided to all other species of tropical fish. A proper aquarium with clean water and a good filtration system is an essential requirement for your betta to achieve its full physical potential and to be happy. And making your betta healthy and happy is what this book is really all about.

AQUATIC TIP

Almost anyone can keep tropical fish, even people who live in apartments or in small homes where other types of pets, such as cats and dogs, are not practical or are prohibited.

After your new aquarium is set up, you can see the effects that good living conditions have on your fish's health by purchasing a betta that is lurking lethargically in a small bowl at your local fish dealer. Next, take the betta home and place it in your well-maintained aquarium. Within a matter of hours, you will notice an increase in coloration, activity level and alertness when your betta happily settles into its new home.

chapter 2

Betta
Basics

Fundamental Fish Anatomy

A betta's life, like that of other species of fish, is dependent upon its body form. A fish's shape, mouth structure and fin design can tell us a lot about the way it lives, eats and moves through the water.

When you gain a basic understanding of how a fish's physical form has evolved to guarantee its survival in different types of aquatic environments, you will be able to look at any new type of species and immediately have a good idea of what its aquarium requirements might be.

What Is a Betta?

A betta is classified as a fish by ichthyologists (people who study fish) because its body form falls into several categories (physical traits) that scientists use to differentiate fish from other types of animals. According to scientists, a bony fish like the betta has a backbone (vertebrae), a brain case (skull) and a small skeleton that protects and supports its body weight and internal organs.

A betta breathes through external gills that are used to extract oxygen from the water. It also has a specialized labyrinth organ that allows the betta to utilize atmospheric air.

Body Shape

The shape of a fish's body can give us several clues to its natural habitat and swimming range. A betta's body is streamlined, allowing it to slip smoothly and effortlessly through open water. The tapered shape lowers the amount of water friction and helps to conserve the betta's energy as it quickly moves to catch its prey. Fish that have a more rounded shape, such as many types of fancy goldfish varieties, are slow swimmers and tire easily.

The slightly flattened or compressed shape of the betta's body is found in fish that live in stagnant or slow-moving waters in their natural habitat. Another example of this type of fish is the discus *(Symphysodon)*, which lives in the Amazon River. Fish that are physically flat on the bottom, such as the cory *(Corydoras)*, tend to spend most of their time hanging near the gravel bed of faster-moving streams.

Mouth Structure

The shape of a fish's mouth is related to the way it feeds and to the range (top, middle, bottom) of water in which it spends most of its time. The betta's mouth is upturned, indicating that it is a top feeder and will scoop up flakes that have fallen onto the water's surface in the aquarium. This is also known as a superior mouth position.

A mouth that is turned down (inferior position) is characteristic of many bottom-dwelling species of fish, such as catfish. These fish feed along the gravel bed and off flat rock surfaces and plant leaves.

When the mouth is facing straight away from the fish's face, it is in the terminal position. This position is common in species, such as guppies and platys, that swim in mid-water levels. These species feed by "picking off" food as it sinks toward the bottom.

Great care should always be taken to ensure that the betta receives its fair share of nourishment, especially if it is living in a tank with

> ## WHEN IS A FISH NOT A FISH?
>
> The definition of exactly what qualifies certain animals in the earth's waters as fish varies quite a bit from person to person. Many people mistakenly believe that all swimming animals—including dolphins and whales—are fish, and do not realize that dolphins and whales are actually mammals because they are warm-blooded and must constantly surface to breathe atmospheric air in order to avoid drowning. To eliminate these misunderstandings, scientists classify animals into groups that have similar physical attributes and functions.

many faster and more aggressive fishes. Just add a little floating food so that your betta will not be forced to compete with mid- and bottom-dwelling species at feeding time.

SCALES

The betta's body is covered with scales that overlap each other like the shingles on the roof of a house. These scales consist of thin, transparent plates that help to protect the betta's body from injury and add streamlining for efficient gliding. A mucus layer covers the scales to provide the betta with extra smoothness (this is the slimy feeling you get when you hold a fish in your hands) and to protect against invading parasites and infection.

There are two main types of scales found in bony fishes: ctenoid and cycloid. *Ctenoid scales* have small teeth on their outer edges, whereas *cycloid scales* are smooth and round like your betta's. The betta's scales grow out from the skin and are generally lacking in color. The betta's true color actually comes from pigment cells that are located in the skin itself.

HEART

A betta's heart is very primitive and contains only two chambers (ventricle and atrium). The heart is located near the front of the betta's body.

SWIM BLADDER

A betta is slightly heavier than water because its skeleton and muscles contain heavy substances that are not generally found in its watery environment. In order to keep from sinking, the betta is equipped with a gas-filled swim bladder that functions as a flotation device.

Through minor, internal gas adjustments using a specialized duct, the betta can remain suspended (neutrally buoyant) with little or no effort. If the betta moves to the bottom of the tank, its swim bladder will be compressed and it will begin to sink. To correct this problem, the betta must either add gas to its swim bladder to achieve neutral buoyancy again or use energy to swim upward.

The opposite is true when the betta moves toward the top of the tank. There, it must release gas from the swim bladder or must use energy to move to a deeper depth. These small changes within the betta's body, unseen by the human eye, are constantly occurring.

FINS

A betta's fins are used not only for propulsion through the water, but for maintaining balance and turning in different directions. The fins are composed of long rays that are surrounded by body tissue and are controlled by muscles. Your betta's fins include one caudal fin (tail), one dorsal fin (located on the upper back region), two pelvic fins (located on the hip area), one anal fin (on the bottom) and two pectoral fins (near the front chest region).

Caudal Fin

The *caudal* (or tail) *fin,* combined with the muscular tail stalk, is primarily responsible for sudden forward movement (bursts of speed) and for fast swimming. In fancy bettas such as the *splendens* varieties, the lengthening of the natural caudal fin through artificial selection (breeding for a specific trait) has resulted in a slower-moving species than its native relative.

A betta uses its fins to maintain its balance, as well as to propel itself through the water.

Dorsal and Anal Fins

The sole purpose of the *dorsal* and *anal fins* is to give the betta stability, in the same manner as the keel on a ship. These fins keep your betta in an upright position. They are critical to prevent it from literally rolling over in the water.

Pectoral Fins

Pectoral fins are used for stability while moving through the water and for turning in different directions. These paired fins are located near the bottom of the betta, directly beneath the gill openings. The pectoral fins can also be used by the male betta to fan its incubating eggs with water.

Pelvic Fins

Pelvic fins aid in body stabilization and in changing directional movement.

COLOR

The betta's color is produced by pigment cells (chromatophores) in the skin. In the wild, a fish uses its coloration to ward off predators and to attract mates.

Wild bettas do not possess the vibrant colors (bright red, lime green, royal blue) of their selectively bred counterparts. However, captive-bred betta males have adopted these new colors and have used them to advantage in mating displays.

The actual colors of a betta are layered. In order

Through selective breeding, different colors are produced. The "bottom" layer of color on a betta is yellow.

to produce a betta of a specific color, other colors that are layered on top must first be "stripped away" through breeding of selective traits. The top color is blue; next is red, then black and finally yellow.

Body Functions

RESPIRATION

A fish's gills are lined with blood vessels that help in respiration. Water is pumped through the mouth and then across the gills where life-giving oxygen is extracted by the gill filaments for use. The remaining water is discarded into the surrounding environment.

Through this process, most fishes can remove up to 85 percent of the oxygen from the water that they take in through the gills. Very active fish, such as danios, must continuously swim forward to force water across their gills in order to obtain enough oxygen for survival. These types of fish will be in a constant state of asphyxiation if placed in a very small aquarium that restricts their free-swimming movement.

A betta's main respiratory device is its *labyrinth organ,* an organ located just behind the gills. The labyrinth organ gets its name from its winding shape, and it absorbs oxygen from the air directly into the blood-stream. However, the betta still extracts a small amount of oxygen from the water by using its gills.

LOCOMOTION

Only a small amount of energy is required by the betta to move through the water. Swimming is very economical (energy efficient) because the betta is supported by the water that surrounds its body. Therefore, very little energy is needed to overcome the force of gravity in water as opposed to that needed by humans on dry land.

Muscle force is achieved through energy created by special fibers in the betta's body. These fibers move in sequence, producing energy in a series of s-shaped curves; this energy is then transferred to the tail. Next, the tail fin pushes the water around it backward, which in turn propels the betta forward.

ORIENTATION IN WATER

A betta will orient itself by sight alone. Any source of light will be interpreted by the betta as meaning "the direction that is up." If you shine a flashlight into the side of a darkened tank, the betta will usually swim sideways in order to reorient itself to its new "up" position.

OSMOSIS

Through the process of osmosis, fish are able to maintain the proper salt levels within their body cells. Freshwater fishes, such as the betta, must keep the salt concentration of their body fluids at a higher level than the salt content of the water in which they live.

Water is continually entering a betta's body through osmosis, and must be removed so that its organs will not burst. Water is removed by the kidneys in the form of a diluted urine. Special salt-absorbing cells located in the gills move sodium chloride (salt) from the water into the blood.

Small amounts of salts that are present in commercial fish foods also help the betta to keep its salt content in balance. The total amount of salt passed into the betta's body is so small that it requires very little energy expenditure to discard.

Marine fish (fish that live in salt water) have the opposite problem. These species must constantly "drink" water to replace that lost to the saltier environment around them. If they do not take in enough extra water, they will eventually die from dehydration.

Senses

VISION

A betta can see in two directions at the same time. This is known as *monocular vision.* It is very difficult for a betta (which can see about a foot away) to focus both of its eyes on a single object.

Instead, the betta relies on its *lateral line* to help it locate objects around it. The lateral line runs down the betta's side from the back of its eye to the base of its tail fin, and is used to detect vibrations in the water. Small holes along the lateral line help to give the betta an "image" of its surroundings, which would otherwise not be visible within the range of its limited eyesight.

A betta is able to detect color visually, but it cannot adjust to rapid light changes, because the iris within its eye works too slowly. That is why a betta will act "shocked" and will panic when an aquarium light is turned on and off without an accompanying change in the room lighting.

A betta moves the lenses of its eyes forward and backward in order to focus.

In humans, the shape and curve of the eye lens is constantly changing in order to achieve proper focus. In a betta's eye, the lens remains the same shape but is moved forward or backward by ligaments for focusing purposes.

Hearing

A betta's ear is composed only of a simple inner chamber because sound in water travels much faster than in air. Vibrations that are picked up from the betta's surrounding environment pass over sensory components to provide sound. Scientists believe that the swim bladder also works together with the betta's inner ear to amplify and distinguish individual sound patterns.

Taste

A betta's taste buds are located on the mouth, lips and fins. The betta's range of taste is very short, so it must constantly forage in hopes of finding food that it needs for survival.

Smell

Smells are taken in through a betta's nostrils, which are connected to its olfactory system. The olfactory system is not joined with the betta's respiratory system, and remains a separate entity.

The Labyrinth Organ

In the wild, bettas live in poorly oxygenated waters, such as swamps and rice paddies. The betta's special labyrinth organ was developed to extract oxygen from the air when needed. The labyrinth is a unique respiratory organ and is found in the suborder *Anabantoidei,* which also includes the paradise fish and the croaking gouramis.

The labyrinth is located inside the head just behind the gill section. This organ consists of rosette-shaped plates containing thousands of blood vessels that absorb oxygen from the atmospheric air that the fish has inhaled. The air is trapped in folds and then absorbed into the betta's bloodstream. The physical shape of this organ is the basis of the name *labyrinth,* which means "maze." Because bettas use oxygen from the air to breathe, they can survive in less space than the average tropical fish can. This allows commercial breeders to keep the males in separate compartments until they are ready to be shipped.

DOES A BETTA SLEEP?

A betta is incapable of closing its eyes, simply because it has no eyelids. Instead, when your betta tires, it will rest either by lying with its abdomen on the gravel or by hanging motionless in the water. This state of suspended animation is accomplished through the use of a swim bladder, and is a sleeping process that requires a short period of time from which to "recover."

Unfortunately, many hobbyists believe that because of this unique physical characteristic, bettas can be kept safely in crowded conditions. Fish keepers must remember that bettas add the same amount of waste to the water that other fishes do, and are just as susceptible to disease brought on by overstocked tanks and poor water conditions.

As mentioned earlier, bettas should never be kept in small bowls for long periods of time. Instead, it is much better to keep them in larger aquariums that contain plenty of swimming space and stable water conditions—it will be much more beneficial to their health in the long run.

Varieties of Bettas

The following betta species are generally available through your local dealer. If a particular species is not available, ask the owner of the fish shop if it can be special-ordered for you.

SARAWAK BETTA (*BETTA AKARENSIS*)

The Sarawak betta has a small, round tail and short fins. The female is usually flat bronze in color. The male can be distinguished by the dark stripe down the length of its side.

PEARLY BETTA (*BETTA ANABATOIDES*)

The pearly betta has a spade-shaped tail and short fins. The female is a dull bronze color with dark splotches, and the male is a brighter bronze with a touch of green appearing on the fins. The male also has a dark stripe that runs straight across from the eyes to the gills.

SLENDER BETTA (*BETTA BELLICA*)

The slender betta has a spade tail and short fins. It is predominantly pink in color. The female has dark dots on the tail and fins. The male has a touch of green over the body and fins. Other colors include orange with a smattering of green or a green-blue with a touch of pink. All have dotted tails and dotted dorsal fins.

EDITH'S BETTA (*BETTA EDITHAE*)

The Edith's betta has a round tail and short fins. The female is dull orange in color with dark splotches and white spots. The male is a brighter orange color with dark splotches. Spots on the male are blue-green and appear in the same physical pattern as the female's.

FOERSHI'S BETTA (*BETTA FOERSHI*)

Foershi's betta has a rounded tail and short fins. The female is pink-orange in color with dark splotches running from front to back. The male is also orange in color. The male's splotches are green, and the gills are bright orange.

21

PEACEFUL BETTA (*BETTA IMBELLIS*)

One of the most commonly kept bettas is the peaceful betta. It has a rounded tail and the fin sizes vary, but the pectoral fins are always long. The body of this betta is predominantly dark with blue-green markings. Its most distinguishing characteristic is that the edge of its tail fin is a bright red. The pectoral fins are red with blue-green tips. The end of the anal fin is red as well. The dorsal fin is almost always a blue-green color. One other significant marking is the appearance of blue-green stripes on the tail.

This pink brunei betta displays the distinctive red stripe in its tail.

BRUNEI BETTA (*BETTA MACROSTOMA*)

The unique pattern found in the brunei betta is a green edging around the dorsal and anal fins. This species has a rounded tail and small fins. Body color can range from gold to pink and white. The white brunei has two dark stripes that run from its head to its tail. The pectoral fins are always green. The pink brunei will have a red stripe in the tail.

THE FIVE MOST POPULAR BETTA SPECIES

1. Fighting Fish *(Betta splendens)*
2. Peaceful Betta *(Betta imbellis)*
3. Emerald Betta *(Betta smaragdina)*
4. Mouthbrooding Betta *(Betta pugnax)*
5. Slender Betta *(Betta bellica)*

PAINTED BETTA (*BETTA PICTA*)

The painted betta has a rounded tail and small fins. This betta is usually gold in color and has three dark stripes that run from head to tail. All fins are edged in green.

MOUTHBROODING BETTA (*BETTA PUGNAX*)

The mouthbrooding betta has a round tail and very small fins. A few have pointed tails. Colors on this fish vary considerably, ranging from a light gray to an orange-gold. Because its colors are so varied, the mouthbrooding betta often looks like it has just finished swimming through a rainbow.

EMERALD BETTA (*BETTA SMARAGDINA*)

The beautiful emerald betta has a rounded tail and very large fins. The body color in this species is usually a deep vibrant green overlaid with a black web design. The long pectoral fins are red in color. The caudal fin is red with green or blue lines. This fish is aptly named due to its vibrant green color.

Note the black web design of the stunning emerald betta.

SIAMESE FIGHTING FISH
(*BETTA SPLENDENS*)

The Siamese fighting fish is the most common betta seen in pet stores today. The caudal fin has a variety of shapes (rounded, pointed, spade, split, double, lace, comb) and is usually long and flowing. The oversized anal fin can range from being cut close to the body, to extending almost three inches in length. The color range of this fish is similar to the selections at a paint store. The large variety of individual color patterns in this species will be discussed shortly.

Siamese fighting fish are known for their long, flowing fins, but some members of the species have relatively short fins.

The unusual combination of pink and orange colors distinguishes Tessy's betta.

Betta splendens is the species most often used in fish shows. It is not unusual for breeders and hobbyists to travel great distances in their search for a betta having a certain color—often for very obscure reasons. I personally know one woman who traveled over 500 miles just to find a *splendens* that would match the color of the drapes in her living room.

BANDED BETTA (*BETTA TAENIATA*)

The banded betta has a round tail and small fins. Colors in this species run from a dull gold to tarnished copper. The body is banded, with flecks of green.

TESSY'S BETTA (*BETTA TESSYAC*)

The Tessy's betta is a unique blend of pink and orange. It also has three dark stripes in a zigzag pattern. The fins on this species have flecks of green throughout.

Betta Color Patterns

There are six major color patterns found in bettas, and these help hobbyists to identify particular variations of a species. As time passes and new strains of bettas are bred, they will be given new pattern names if they do not fit into the existing categories. The following descriptions should give you an idea of what to look for when you are searching for a particular pattern. Note that many hobbyists and breeders disagree on exact pattern definitions.

SOLID-COLORED BETTA

A solid-colored betta will have one color (bright red, royal blue, orange or gold) that basically covers the entire body and fin areas. There are generally flaws in the solidness of the color (small specks of white and the like), which breeders are working to eliminate.

BICOLORED BETTA

A bicolored betta has a body that is one solid color, with fins that are a lighter or darker variation of the same color. For example, a betta with a light blue body and dark blue fins would be considered bicolored.

A betta with body and fins of different coloration is known as a Cambodian betta.

CAMBODIAN BETTA

A Cambodian betta has a body of one color and fins of another. For example, the body on this type may be red, with all fins carrying a light blue color.

25

Butterfly Betta

A butterfly betta has a body of one color that blends into the fins near the torso area. The outer edges of the fins are a different color.

Cambodian-Butterfly Betta

The Cambodian-butterfly betta, as its name suggests, is a cross between a Cambodian and a butterfly betta. The body on this betta will be of one color, whereas the fins will carry two different colors. For example, the Cambodian-butterfly can have a red body with blue and gold fins.

Marbled Betta

A marbled betta is unique. The body and the fin tips are the same color. The inner portion of the fins are a different color, which gives this type the appearance of being striped.

Tankmates for Bettas

Guppies adjust well to different water conditions.

Despite the fact that male bettas fight viciously among themselves, a single male betta rarely bothers other fishes in the community aquarium. Bettas can be successfully kept with most peaceful species of fish. The following list offers a few suggestions for betta tankmates that I have personally found acceptable. Remember, however, there is invariably a "bad apple" in every group, and your results may vary depending on your individual fish's temperament. An observant eye and a little experimentation will give you the results that you are looking for.

Common Guppy (*Poecilia reticulata*)

The guppy comes in many different strains of color that will make an attractive addition to your betta tank.

The male of this species is much more colorful than the female. However, females are now being offered that have small amounts of coloring and stripes on the fins and rear section of the body.

Guppies do best in a tank that is heavily planted. This species is very flexible on temperature and pH requirements, and will eat almost any food that is offered. Guppies grow to a length of 1½ inches and bear fully formed live young. Guppies have been known to change sex depending on the environmental need.

The platy is considered by some to be the ideal community fish.

PLATY (*XIPHOPHORUS MACULATUS*)

The platy is a beautiful variety of fish that can be found in almost any color under the rainbow. This species is very hardy and peaceful. The platy bears live young and is not very picky about what it eats. Platys reach lengths of 2 inches and do well in warmer waters.

Swordtails are known for their long caudal fin.

SWORDTAIL (*XIPHOPHORUSS*)

The swordtail is similar in appearance to the platy but has a body that looks like a torpedo. The males of this

All About Bettas

species have an extended caudal fin that resembles a sword. Often females will change sex to become males as they mature. The swordtail will eat a wide variety of foods and will grow to a length of 4 inches. Swordtails bear live young.

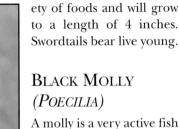

BLACK MOLLY (*POECILIA*)

A molly is a very active fish but will generally leave its tankmates unmolested if the tank is planted with adequate fauna. This fish enjoys a slightly higher temperature and therefore will be very compatible with the betta's requirements. The molly needs plenty of vegetable matter in its diet, so take this into consideration at feeding time. This species attains a length of 2½ inches and bears live young. Mollies are available in a wide variety of patterns, such as marble and dalmation, and can also sport sailfins.

Because the black molly likes water on the warm side, it makes a nice tankmate for your betta.

WHITE CLOUD (*TANICHTHYS ALBONUBES*)

The white cloud mountain minnow is a very hardy species that carries blue and red iridescent bands along the length of its body. This fish tolerates a wide range of temperatures, and will swim near the upper levels of the tank. The white cloud will eat almost any food offered and is very peaceful.

The peaceful white cloud mountain minnow will eat almost anything.

CORY (*CORYDORAS*)

The cory is great for cleaning debris from the bottom of the tank, and it also serves a useful function by eating unwanted algae. This species bears several types of interesting patterns ranging from spots to zigzags. For most of the day, the cory stays near the lower levels of the tank. However, it can occasionally be seen shooting toward the surface with quick bursts of speed. This species is not aggressive and will do well with your bettas. Corys grow to an average length of 2 inches.

GLASS CATFISH (*KRYPTOPTERUS BICIRRHUS*)

The glass catfish is a fascinating fish that is almost transparent. The internal organs of this species can be seen through the body. This species will stay near the mid-levels of the tank. The glass catfish is very peaceful and will make an exciting addition to the betta tank.

Members of the Corydoras species tend to be hardy and will clean up debris at the bottom of the tank (Corydoras un-dulatus).

Setting
Up

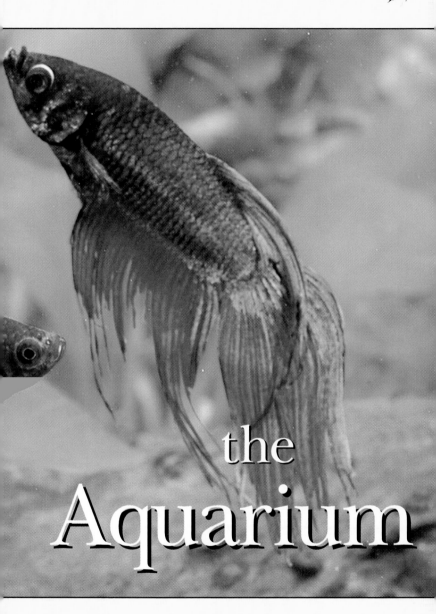

the
Aquarium

chapter 3

The **Tank** and Its Components

There are many factors to consider before purchasing an aquarium tank. You may want to put your aquarium in an area of your home where everyone would enjoy it, or perhaps you think that placing it in a quieter area would be best. Factors such as cost, other family members and space considerations will have a large bearing on your final decision. Another variable that has to be weighed carefully is the total number of other aquariums you are planning to purchase in the future.

Financial Considerations

The aquarium tank is the most important piece of fishkeeping equipment that you will ever own, so purchase the best quality tank within your budget. Remember that all other hardware, such as filters and heaters, must fit into or on your new tank, and don't forget to add these items into your final total when calculating your financial limits.

In deciding which tank to buy, you must take into account the tank's size. Larger tanks require larger equipment, which in turn will cost a little more than the same hardware for a smaller aquarium. If you take the time to make a few quick trips to your local fish dealer, these information-gathering excursions will give you a good general idea of how much each particular setup will cost.

After the aquarium is completely set up and running, bear in mind that you will also need to purchase additional equipment such as nets, extra filtration medium, test kits, an aquarium vacuum and a variety of medications just in case one of your fish happens to contract a disease.

The good news is that aquariums provide excellent overall value for your hard-earned money, and generally cost less than many other types of domestic pets. The small financial outlay at the beginning will pay you back a hundredfold in years to come by giving you unending enjoyment and pleasure.

Space Considerations

An important factor to consider when choosing your aquarium is the amount of free space that you will have for the tank. If you live in a small apartment, for example, a 10- or 20-gallon tank aquarium may be the size that will suit your needs best. If you live in a large home, you may have a little more area to work with, and you might be able to purchase a bigger tank, such as a 40- or 55-gallon one, without cramping your living space.

The following table will give you a general idea of the minimum space requirements (length by width by height) that several standard-size aquarium tanks will require.

Tank Capacity	Tank Shape	Dimensions
10 Gallon	Regular	$20 \times 10 \times 12$
	Long	$24 \times 8 \times 12$
15 Gallon	Regular	$24 \times 12 \times 12$
	Long	$20 \times 10 \times 18$
	Show	$24 \times 8 \times 16$
20 Gallon	High	$24 \times 12 \times 16$
	Long	$30 \times 12 \times 12$
25 Gallon	Regular	$24 \times 12 \times 20$
30 Gallon	Regular	$36 \times 12 \times 16$
	Breeding	$36 \times 18 \times 12$
40 Gallon	Long	$48 \times 13 \times 16$
	Breeding	$36 \times 18 \times 16$
45 Gallon	Regular	$36 \times 12 \times 24$
50 Gallon	Regular	$36 \times 18 \times 18$
55 Gallon	Regular	$48 \times 13 \times 20$
65 Gallon	Regular	$36 \times 18 \times 24$
75 Gallon	Regular	$48 \times 18 \times 20$

Where to Place an Aquarium

Place the aquarium in an area of your home that is free from cold drafts and direct sunlight in order to keep the water in the tank from overheating or chilling. Thus, such rooms as basements (unless well-insulated and heated) and garages and locations near windows and doors are not good choices. Avoid a space that is drafty or where the temperature changes rapidly and unexpectedly.

Number of Tanks

When planning your fishkeeping hobby, you must also decide whether you are going to keep only one aquarium or whether you plan on expanding your hobby at a later date to accommodate more tanks. If you want to keep several male bettas at a time, you might consider purchasing a few smaller tanks instead of buying just one large aquarium that would require a divider.

A larger tank would be more suitable for use as a community aquarium with a single betta and several peaceful tankmates.

Types of Tanks

Today's extensive retail aquarium market offers a host of superior products. The heavy metal frames on earlier designs were subject to rust—if the tank was holding saltwater, the aquarium salt would eventually corrode the metal and become toxic to the inhabitants of the tank.

For a healthy home for your fish, you will need to invest in a good tank, filter and aeration systems, as well as some decorations and plants.

GLASS TANKS

Today, all-glass aquariums are the most popular of all tanks. These aquariums are made of plate glass and are sealed with a nontoxic silicone that allows for expansion when the tank is filled with water. Glass tanks are very resistant to scratching and will give you a good viewing area because of the flatness of the front, back and side walls. One disadvantage of glass aquariums, as compared with acrylic aquariums, is the difficulty of drilling holes in the glass for filter parts, something that is easily accomplished with acrylic tanks.

Glass tanks are also much heavier than acrylic tanks and can be difficult to move, especially when the tank is large. Large glass tanks are extremely heavy because the glass used in construction gets increasingly thicker as the tank size gets larger to combat water pressure problems. Of course, the main drawback to glass aquariums is the possibility that they may break or shatter, leaving you with a huge mess to clean up.

PLASTIC TANKS

Plastic tanks are very inexpensive, but they have several serious drawbacks. These types of tanks scratch easily and tend to discolor with age. Most plastic tanks are available only in small sizes (2- and 5-gallon) and really do not provide the proper space and surface area needed to keep a successful aquarium.

ACRYLIC TANKS

Acrylic tanks are increasingly available in pet shops and through magazine advertisements. These fantastic lightweight tanks can be found in a large number of amazing shapes and sizes, such as bubble and convex.

BUILDING YOUR OWN TANK

Avoid the temptation to build your own tank unless you really know how to make a secure and safe aquarium. Working with glass can be dangerous, and it is much better to purchase a tank than to flirt with water leaks and other such disasters that often accompany aquariums built by inexperienced hobbyists.

The disadvantages of acrylic aquariums are that they are a little bit more expensive than all-glass tanks and are easily scratched. However, there are several good scratch remover products on the market that will easily cover most simple blemishes caused by cleaning and carelessness.

An acrylic tank will also have a small amount of visual distortion, which is due to the bending of the material during construction. These bends, however, give the tank a "seamless" look that is very appealing. Glass tanks, in contrast, force the hobbyist to view the fish by looking around thickly formed corners.

TANK SHAPES

Acrylic aquariums can be molded into a number of fascinating shapes, including rectangles, squares, hexagons, octagons, tubes, fish-eyes, bubbles, L-shapes and several other unique styles that will satisfy the individual tastes and space limitations of each buyer. When choosing the shape of your tank, however, there are several concerns to keep in mind.

An aquarium's shape affects the amount of oxygen that its water will contain on a continuous basis. Vital gas ex-change (carbon dioxide for oxygen) occurs at the water surface. A tall, narrow tank with a small surface area will accommodate much less gas exchange than a shorter tank having a longer and larger surface area.

Tank shape also affects your betta's free-swimming area. In the wild, bettas are found in shallow pools that have more width than depth. Accordingly, a standard rectangular-style aquarium will not only provide good surface area for gas exchange, but allow sufficient swimming space as well.

Gas exchange is enhanced by a large surface area. The surface-to-air ratio of a long tank is much larger than that of a bowl or a tall, narrow tank.

The number of fish that you will be able to safely keep in your new aquarium will also depend on the tank's shape. Once again, it is the total surface area of the aquarium that determines the number of fish that it can hold.

Tank Size

A freshwater tank should never be smaller than 10 gallons to ensure that your new fish have an adequate surface area for stable water conditions. A 20-gallon tank is a good starting size for almost any hobbyist. The larger the surface area and volume of the tank, the more stable the water conditions will be.

Large tanks also provide stability in water temperature and nutrient mix. A shallow tank with increased length is biologically desirable for the absorption of oxygen and dissipation of carbon dioxide at the surface, and these conditions are beneficial to your betta.

Tank Weight

The weight of the tank is an important factor in deciding which tank to purchase. Fresh water weighs about 8 pounds per gallon. For example, after adding just the water, a 200-gallon tank would weigh roughly 1,600 pounds without equipment! Make sure you provide your new tank with a sturdy stand and distribute the weight of the tank as evenly as possible over strong flooring.

COMPLETE AQUARIUM WEIGHT

To give you a better idea of how much a fully loaded aquarium (including fish, gravel, equipment and the like) will weigh, you can use the following formula by simply measuring the sides and height of the tank:

$$\text{Capacity in Gallons} = \frac{\text{Length} \times \text{Width} \times \text{Height (in inches)}}{232}$$

For example, a 10-gallon tank that measures 20 inches in length, by 10 inches in width, by 12 inches in height would weigh approximately 100 pounds.

HOW MANY GALLONS DOES A TANK HOLD?

On some of the older tanks, it can be difficult to find information on exactly how many gallons the aquarium will hold. Aquarium tank sizes have become fairly standard, but many odd-sized tanks that were manufactured years ago are still available secondhand. It is possible that you may run across one of these older tanks and need to figure out how many gallons it holds. A good formula for obtaining gallon capacity of an aquarium is as follows:

$$\frac{Length \times Width \times Height}{231}$$

For example, a tank measuring measures 24 inches in length, by 12 inches in width, by 16 inches in height would contain approximately 20 gallons. This formula is very useful if you happen to run across a tank at a garage sale or auction.

Buying Secondhand

If you decide to purchase a secondhand tank, be sure to carefully inspect your purchase for leaks, cracks and silicone wear. When buying used tanks from a retailer, check to see if the silicone seal is complete and un-interrupted. Even a small break in this seal can even-

To keep your fish (and your home) safe, be sure to carefully check the seal on a used tank.

tually cause leaking. An aquarium with old sealer can, however, be salvaged. Simply remove the old sili-cone with a razor (please exercise great care when using a sharp instrument!) and then replace it with new sealer. Allow the new sealer to dry for at least 48 hours before you add any water to the tank.

Ready for Setup
PLACEMENT OF THE STAND

The first step in setting up an aquarium is to place the stand in its permanent position. The stand should be constructed of a solid material capable of holding at least 100 pounds more than the total weight of your aquarium. This extra allotment for weight will keep your stand from buckling over a long period of time.

Stands that include a built-in cabinet are great for storing unsightly equipment and chemicals. An aquarium should fit its stand correctly; none of the tank should hang over the sides. A stand that is too small can cause a tank to warp or break.

The aquarium stand that you choose should be placed on a solid surface. If you live in an apartment, mobile home or old house, always check the floor and its supports so that your brand-new aquarium does not go through the floor. Avoid using expensive household furniture as an aquarium stand, because any unforeseen water leaks can ruin the finish quickly.

ELECTRICAL CONSIDERATIONS

When you are siting your aquarium, keep in mind that you will need access to a few electrical outlets. I have known hobbyists who have set up their complete aquarium system and then added water, only to find out that there was no electrical plug anywhere near the tank!

An electrical strip with four to five outlets works great for an aquarium system. With a strip, you can connect several pieces of equipment and use only half of one wall outlet. Try to find an electrical strip that has a built-in circuit breaker. This will prevent expensive damage to your equipment from power surges and electrical storms.

Do *not* connect outlets to a wall switch. Disaster can strike if all the equipment is turned off because someone accidentally hit the switch. A word of caution: Never attempt to wire aquarium equipment or wall sockets yourself. Contact a professional if an electrical problem occurs.

> ### MOVING YOUR TANK
>
> *Never* attempt to move a full aquarium no matter how large or small it may be. A slight shift in weight and water pressure is all that is required to break the glass. An aquarium should always be moved by at least two people. Always lift an aquarium by placing your hands underneath the bottom corners of the tank.

PREFILL CLEANING

Once you have the stand in place, it is time to clean your aquarium tank. Never use any type of soap products;

they can leave a residue along the glass that can be lethal to your fish. A little bit of warm water and a stiff sponge will remove any film or dirt on the tank. If the tank is used and has a lime buildup on the glass, this can be removed with an aquarium scraper. After your tank has been thoroughly cleaned, it is ready to be placed on the stand.

Supporting and Placing Your Tank

When you set up your new tank, be sure to add a thin layer of Styrofoam beneath the bottom for support; the Styrofoam will compensate for any irregularities in the aquarium's bottom surface. Do not forget to leave room between the tank and the wall for any equipment, such as power filters, that will hang from the backside. A good aquarium will have a half-inch countersunk frame on top to support the cover glass or hood. This countersink will help to prevent water from spilling out.

A "homey" environment will make your betta comfortable. Choose a substrate with a natural color.

Substrate

The substrate or gravel in your tank plays an important role in the biological cycle. Beneficial bacteria grow along the top of the gravel bed and will help to break

41

down waste in the aquarium. Gravel is also useful for anchoring live plants and holding down decorations.

Note that brightly colored or neon gravel competes with the natural beauty of your betta. In addition, your fish will feel much more comfortable in a natural-looking environment. A "homey" environment helps to reduce stress and will promote spawning and other natural behaviors.

Substrate Size

Substrates are available in a variety of sizes and shapes. Large-grained materials should be avoided because food can get trapped between the granules, causing the water to become foul, even in a short period of time.

Small-grained substrates (sand) will quickly clog the water flow and cause a rise in unwanted *anaerobic bacteria* (bacteria that thrive without oxygen). If sand is used, it should be laid down in a very thin layer. Note that some betta tankmates, such as corys, prefer a sandier substrate over coarse gravel (the coarse gravel can damage their delicate mouth tissues). A thin layer of sand would suit these fish nicely. On the whole, however, it is wisest to choose a medium-grade substrate.

How Much Substrate Do I Need?

The amount of substrate required for a freshwater tank varies not only with the aquarium size, but also with the type of filtration used. If an undergravel filter is used, a 2- to 3-inch layer of substrate will be needed. If an undergravel filter is not used, only 1 inch of substrate should cover the bottom of the tank. Without an undergravel filter, other sizes of substrate may be used safely. On the average, an aquarium will need about 1½ pounds of substrate per gallon.

Adding Substrate

Wash all gravel before adding it to your tank. To clean the gravel, place it in a large bucket and run water over it while you mix it up with your hand or a large spoon.

Continue to wash the gravel until the water that is running off it is completely clean.

Gravel and sand should be sloped from back to front so that a deeper depth is maintained toward the rear glass. This arrangement will help to filter waste material and uneaten food toward the front of the tank where it can be easily vacuumed. The substrate in the back of the tank should be about one-half inch higher than the front. Rock can also be placed in layers toward the back of the tank so that wastes and debris will slide toward the front of the tank where they can easily be seen.

Decorations
ROCKS

If you add rocks to your aquarium, be sure to embed them in the gravel so that they touch the undergravel plate. Scooping up excess gravel around each rock will help to keep the rock from sliding down on top of your fish. Never lean rocks up against the glass for support, because they can fall and injure your betta or break the sides of the tank. Make sure that all rocks have a smooth surface to prevent injury.

One way to create a permanent and safe effect is to glue rocks together using a silicone aquarium sealer. This will keep your rock display in place should burrowing bottom dwellers begin to dig around them. Always allow the sealer to dry for 24 hours before you place the rocks in the aquarium.

WOOD

Large pieces of driftwood often make great centerpieces for an aquarium. It is best to buy pretreated wood from an aquarium shop. Pieces of wood that are obtained from an outside environment carry the risk of introducing bacteria and unwanted pests into your tank.

For this reason, all such "environmentally obtained" wood should be cleaned with warm water and sealed with two coats of aquarium-safe polyurethane varnish before being added to the tank. The varnish will seal the wood completely and prevent the release of any organisms that still remain within it.

Pieces of driftwood add to a tank's beauty. If you want to add wood, it is best to obtain pretreated wood from your dealer.

BACKGROUNDS

Backgrounds can be very important to your betta. A natural background depicting an open stream or plant bed is best. A solid color background will work well if no other type can be found. Even aluminum foil can be added to the back of the tank and shaped to achieve an interesting "cave-like" look. Backgrounds will help to eliminate movement and shadow that can frighten your betta and will provide it with a little extra security.

Water Quality

Once you have placed the substrate and a few decorations into the tank, it is time to add water to your aquarium. Water is the most important element in an aquarium setup. A few conditions must be met so that the water in your tank will suit your betta's physical and environmental needs. Standard aquarium equipment and a few simple test kits are all that are needed to ensure that water conditions remain optimal.

TEMPERATURE

In the betta's natural habitat of the Orient, warm water conditions prevail. Therefore, the water temperature in a betta's aquarium should be maintained near 80°F.

Loss of appetite, lethargy, disease and starvation often occur when bettas are kept in cooler temperatures. A good air supply, such as a large bubble disk, will distribute the warm water throughout the tank and prevent "cold pockets" from occurring.

If the proper temperature is maintained, you will quickly notice that your fish will be alert, feed ravenously and display brilliant color. A cold betta will lurk in corners, clamp its fins and remain inactive.

Despite the fact that bettas can breathe oxygen, they are just as sensitive to poor water conditions as other tropicals. Keeping a betta in a tiny bowl does not provide your fish with a healthy environment. High nitrates and ammonia levels can rapidly damage the betta's labyrinth organ and gills. Poor water conditions can stress a betta and cause ich, velvet, and other bacterial diseases.

CHLORINE

City water departments add chlorine and chloramine to drinking water to eliminate harmful bacteria and to make it safe for human consumption. However, these chemicals can be deadly to your aquarium pets and must be removed. Bottled chlorine remover, purchased at your local pet shop, will neutralize chlorine and chloramine from your tap water. Many of these dechlorinators also enhance the natural slime coat of your fish. Simply follow the label's directions, and add the chemical to the water before any fish or live plants are put into the aquarium.

Another way to remove chlorine is to aerate the water for 12 hours or let it sit in open jugs for 48 hours. Filters containing activated carbon (power filters, corner filters and the like) will remove chlorine from the tap water in a day's time.

pH VALUES

The *pH* (a measure of alkalinity or acidity) in aquarium water should be checked when you first set up

your tank and then checked afterward on a regular
basis. In a freshwater system such as your betta tank,
pH values can fluctuate rapidly. Even small changes in
pH can stress your betta and make it more susceptible
to various types of diseases.

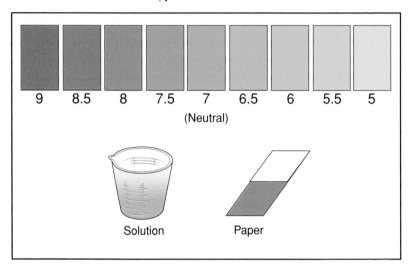

| 9 | 8.5 | 8 | 7.5 | 7 | 6.5 | 6 | 5.5 | 5 |

(Neutral)

Solution   Paper

*Test the pH of
your aquarium
water with sim-
ple kits available
at your dealer.*

A pH scale ranges from 0 to 14. Zero is the lowest value
on the scale and the highest acidic level. Fourteen is
the highest value on the scale and the highest level of
alkalinity. A pH of 7 is halfway between acidity and
alkalinity and is considered neutral.

Your betta will prefer water with a pH between 6.5
(slightly acidic) and 7 (neutral). Most other fish that
would make good betta tankmates can live comfortably
within this particular range.

The pH in your aquarium can be measured with simple test kits available at almost any pet store. Most kits
consist of a color card, plastic measuring tube and
chemicals. These kits are quite simple to use.

If the pH of the water is too high (alkaline), it can be
lowered by using the chemicals in the test kit or by
adding demineralized water. Another way to lower the
pH is to filter the water through peat moss.

If the pH of the water is too low (acidic), it can be
raised by adding chemicals from the test kit, soaking

the water in dolomite or coral pieces, or running the water through limestone that has been added to a mechanical filter.

If there are any fish in your aquarium, the pH must be changed gradually. Changes of more than one range value per day can shock your fish and result in death.

Water Hardness

The *dH* (degree of hardness) is simply the amount of dissolved mineral salts in the aquarium water. One way to dilute hardness is to add rain or distilled water to your tank. This will also lower the pH. Extreme hardness is found in alkaline (high pH) water. Bettas prefer soft water that has a dH of less than 25. Reverse osmosis units will also soften aquarium water, but they are expensive and use a lot of tap water to produce a small amount of mineral-free water.

The nitrogen cycle.

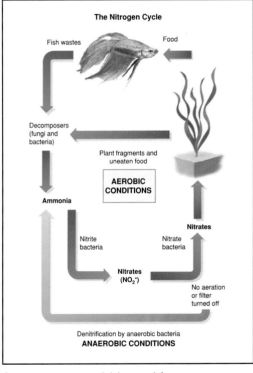

The Nitrogen Cycle

Fish wastes

Food

Decomposers
(fungi and
bacteria)

Plant fragments and
uneaten food

**AEROBIC
CONDITIONS**

Ammonia

Nitrite
bacteria

Nitrate
bacteria

Nitrates

**Nitrates
(NO₂⁻)**

No aeration
or filter
turned off

Denitrification by anaerobic bacteria
ANAEROBIC CONDITIONS

Nitrogen Cycle

With any new aquarium, it is vitally important to condition (age) your tank water to provide your new acquisitions with the best possible chance of survival.

When new fish are added to your tank, ammonia will begin to build up as it is excreted through their waste. Proper biological filtration is required to convert this deadly ammonia into less potent nitrites and then later into safer nitrates. This is accomplished through bacteria that matures during the nitrogen cycle.

During the conditioning process, several types of bacteria multiply rapidly over a period of months in order to remove toxic chemicals from the water. As the number of bacteria increases, larger amounts of waste products are rendered less toxic through biochemical conversions in the nitrogen cycle.

Ammonia also accumulates in a new aquarium through excretion and decay of nitrogen products such as fish food. Eventually, as the aquarium ages, nitrates will build up to the point where they can begin to affect your fish's health. The best way to remove nitrates is to change the water frequently.

CONDITIONING TIME

Conditioning time varies depending on the temperature of the water and the type and number of filtration units used. This period may take anywhere from three weeks to several months. The process will begin only after your starter fish have been introduced into the tank. A few hardy species, such as guppies or a single betta, should be added to the new aquarium to start the conditioning of the biological filter.

Ammonia levels begin to peak within 7 to 14 days, and eventually the nitrosomonas bacteria increase to detoxify the ammonia into nitrites. Next, the nitrites will accumulate into higher levels, and nitrobacter bacteria will begin to convert them to nitrates. Eventually, nitrite levels drop and the conditioning period ends. Nitrate levels will continue to slowly increase over time but can be maintained at proper levels through frequent water changes.

MONITORING WATER CONDITIONS

During the conditioning period, pH, ammonia, nitrite and nitrate levels should be monitored daily using standard test kits. The pH should remain within the 6.5 to 7 range. Note that the pH will drop during the conditioning process, but you can raise it by using frequent water changes if you have hard water.

Allowing the pH to reduce for long periods of time during the conditioning process will hinder the bacteria from multiplying to their full potential. When nitrite and nitrate levels begin to overstep their own limits, daily water changes will also help to alleviate that problem.

Chemicals and medications should not be used in excess during the conditioning period, as they can potentially damage bacterial growth.

Adding Fish

After the conditioning process is complete, you can begin adding a few fish every few weeks to allow the bacteria bed to increase at a normal rate. If you make the mistake of immediately overstocking your aquarium, you will begin to notice a gradual buildup in ammonia levels again. To correct this situation, the number of fish in the tank must be reduced, or more filtration must be added to efficiently process the increased load of ammonia.

Add new fish slowly to maintain the proper water chemistry in your tank.

With a little patience, the conditioning period of your aquarium can be easily accomplished without any unnecessary loss of life. A few simple principles are all that are needed to maintain water properly in your aquarium.

chapter 4

Understanding Equipment

Filtration Systems

Filters play an essential role in the biological cycle of your betta's aquarium. Some filters, depending on construction, can perform mechanical, chemical and biological functions all at the same time. The main functions of your filtration system are to promote the nitrogen cycle and remove debris from the water. Because most models release water bubbles, they also aerate the water.

BIOLOGICAL FILTRATION

Biological filtration supplies a substrate on which nitrifying bacteria can colonize. Nitrifying bacteria convert deadly ammonia that is produced by fish waste and food debris to nitrites and nitrates. This biological purification process is also known as *detoxification* or the *nitrogen cycle*.

Chemical Filtration

Chemical filtration is the adsorption of molecular compounds through filter mediums to cleanse impurities in the water. This filtration takes place on mediums such as activated charcoal and zeolite, that absorb chemicals and dissolved minerals as water is passed over them before it is returned to the tank.

Mechanical Filtration

Mechanical filtration uses materials such as fiber floss, foam or sponges to capture small particles of dirt and debris that pass through the materials. Over time, the surface areas of all these mediums become covered with beneficial bacteria, and they are then able to perform biological filtration.

Corner/Box Filter

Major Functions: Biological, Mechanical, Chemical

The corner filter is one of the oldest systems in the aquarium hobby. Originally designed for small aquariums, a corner filter is generally shaped like a box and contains a single airstone attached to a pump that pushes water through layers of activated charcoal and floss. The filter itself rests on the gravel bed inside the tank.

Corner filters are inefficient in cleaning large volumes of water, have a low turnover rate, can be very noisy and will often float around the tank if not weighted down properly. With the availability of more efficient, electrically powered filters, this type of filter is becoming obsolete.

Power Filter

Major Functions: Biological, Chemical, Mechanical

A boxed power filter is powered by electricity and hangs on the back of the aquarium tank. Power filters come in a wide variety of sizes, and usually have one or two slots that hold fiber pads containing charcoal.

Water is sucked up through an intake tube, passed over the filter pads and then gently rolled back onto the water surface. The pads on these filters are easy to replace and simple to clean.

UNDERGRAVEL FILTER

Major Functions: Biological, Chemical

The undergravel filter is one of the best systems made for creating good biological filtration. This type of filter consists of one or more perforated plastic plates that sit about an inch above the bottom of the aquarium. Two to six hard plastic uplift tubes are inserted into holes in the base plates and are connected to an air pump by tubing and airstones.

The aquarium gravel and other substrates act as the biological filter medium for this type of system. Water flows down through the bacteria bed that is colonized on the gravel, and is then passed through an airspace underneath the plate before being returned up the tubes and over charcoal inserts and back into the tank itself.

An undergravel filter creates good biological filtration by moving water through the bacteria bed on the gravel.

A *reverse-flow undergravel filter* draws water through a mechanical filter and then passes it back down the uplift tubes to be distributed throughout the aquarium after it is pushed up through the gravel bed. A reverse-flow

52

system increases the efficiency of the undergravel filter and longevity of the bacterial colony.

Powerhead

A powerhead is a square pump that is sealed in hard plastic and is powered by electricity. Powerheads can be inserted into undergravel uplift tubes to increase the filter's output and efficiency. Powerheads also have adjustable valves to regulate the speed of the airflow, and can be turned to direct the waterflow to certain areas of your aquarium.

SAFETY FIRST

When cleaning your tank or rearranging the décor, *always* unplug all electrical equipment.

CANISTER FILTER

Major Functions: Biological, Chemical, Mechanical

A canister filter contains several media compartments through which the aquarium water is drawn at high pressure by means of a pump. These units are capable of turning over up to 900 gallons per hour. A canister filter can be attached to the back of the aquarium glass, or connected by long hoses. This is one of the most efficient filters on the market for larger aquariums and is well worth the investment.

FLUIDIZED BED FILTER

Major Function: Biological

A fluidized bed filter is extremely compact and uses sand as its filter medium. The sand greatly increases the surface area on which beneficial bacteria can grow and multiply. Oxygenation is improved with this type of filtration system because the internal sand is constantly being tumbled in water, creating a "fluidized bed." The sand grains fall through the water, resulting in an excellent transfer capability between the water and the bacterial film that is present on the media.

A fluidized bed filter will respond quickly to extreme changes in ammonia levels caused by overstocking and overfeeding.

SPONGE FILTER

Major Function: Biological

A sponge filter draws aquarium water through a large sponge that acts as a biological medium as bacteria gather on its surface. This type of filter is often used in quarantine, hospital and fry tanks.

Aeration

In the wild, bettas live in stagnant water. They do, however, seem to adapt to most of the aeration that is released by standard filtration systems. Nonetheless, aeration in the aquarium should not be so overpowering that your betta is forced to expend all of its energy fighting strong currents. An aquarium that is heavily planted and has undergravel tubes that reach the surface of the water will help to break up some of the stronger turbulence.

By including a number of plants in the tank, you can diminish the strength of water currents caused by the filter and aerators.

AIR PUMPS

Air pumps can be purchased in both vibrator and piston models. Air pumps drive air though tubes where the air is then broken into smaller bubbles as it passes into an airstone or filter. Your air pump should sit above the aquarium level, if possible, to avoid any backflow of water if the power is shut off.

Standard vibrator pumps are not as expensive as piston pumps and require little maintenance, but they can be quite noisy. Piston pumps are more powerful than vibrator pumps but need to be oiled and require special traps to keep the oil from getting into the aquarium.

AIRSTONES

Airstones increase oxygenation by dispersing the air supplied by the pump. Airstones are usually made of perforated ceramic or wood-based materials.

Tubing

Aquarium tubing has a variety of uses, including connecting such equipment as airstones in an undergravel filter and bubble discs to the air pump.

The new tubing on the market is made of a silicone/ rubber material and is easy to work with. This tubing has been colored blue-green by the manufacturer and blends in nicely with the tint of the aquarium water. Rubber tubing is easy to bend and weave around decorations and does not crack with age.

Heaters

Submersible aquarium heaters have a watertight glass tube containing an electrical element that is wound around a ceramic core. A small light indicates whether the heater is on or off. A temperature adjustment value allows you to easily change the range of your heater by choosing a temperature located on an internal thermometer. *Nonsubmersible heaters* hang on the tank's frame, with the glass tube resting in the water. These types of heaters generally do not have a thermometer attached.

If you are using only one submersible heater, it should be placed in a horizontal position on the center of the aquarium glass in the rear, so that heat will flow evenly throughout the tank. Ideally, two heaters should be operating at the same time, just in case one happens to fail.

A general rule of thumb for determining heater size is to allow 5 watts of heater per gallon. So, a 20-gallon aquarium would need a heater that is at least 100 watts.

THERMOMETERS

Thermometers are inexpensive and are available in three basic varieties.

The stick-on thermometer is completely flat and has a peel-off backing. This type of thermometer is usually applied to the outside glass near a corner. Individual degree panels light up as the water temperature changes.

A second type of thermometer is one that can be hung from the tank frame on the inside of the aquarium glass. The temperature is shown through a capillary tube containing mercury that moves up or down. The highest point in the mercury line displays the current temperature. Be aware that this type of thermometer can be moved easily by the fish in your tank and the water current.

The best type of thermometer is similar to the hanging version, except that it has a small suction cup that holds it firmly in place against the inside glass. All thermometers should be placed in an area where they are easy to read and do not block your overall view.

Because bettas do best in warm water, a good heater and thermometer are a must.

Lighting

Your betta will need a cycle of day (lighting) and night (darkness) to imitate the conditions of its native habitat. Light plays an important role in your betta's internal biological clock, which determines feeding and spawning patterns. Your aquarium lighting should never be left on overnight for this very reason.

FLUORESCENT BULBS

Fluorescent lighting is a good choice for the betta aquarium. It fosters plant growth, has a long lamp life, does not produce a lot of heat, has an even spectrum of light and is offered in a wide variety of colors. These lights tend to lose a portion of their power after about seven months, and should be replaced at that time.

ACTINIC BLUE BULBS

Actinic blue bulbs produce long-wave ultraviolet radiation that is good for plant growth. However, use of these bulbs will also produce an abundance of algae.

METAL HALIDE LIGHTS

Metal halide lights have an improved yellow and red output, and produce an aquarium effect that it is pleasing to the human eye. The only drawback to this type of system is that they are very expensive.

MERCURY VAPOR LIGHTS

Mercury vapor lights are high powered and generally used for lighting tanks that are very deep. Mercury vapor lights lack green and blue wavelengths and require supplemental lighting to achieve full spectrum. These lights are usually suspended over the tank.

> **AVOID INCANDESCENT LIGHTING FOR YOUR TANK**
>
> Tungsten (incandescent) lighting is generally found in the standard light bulbs that are used in your home's lamps. It is *not* suitable for the aquarium: it has a short lamp life, produces too much heat, has uneven output and has a limited spectrum.

Mercury vapor lights are very economical because they retain up to 90 percent of their original capacity even after several years of use.

Other Equipment

HOODS

Aquarium hoods come in one of two styles. A *full hood* is cast as one complete piece that includes the lighting fixture. A *split hood* often has a complete glass cover with a separate lighting unit.

Hoods should be tight fitting to keep your fish from jumping out of the tank and to keep dust and debris from entering the water. Make sure that you follow the manufacturer's instructions on maximum lighting wattage to avoid melting the unit with a bulb that is too powerful.

AQUARIUM CLAW

An aquarium claw is a handy tool that is made of hard plastic and is used for picking up items in an aquarium. This tool usually has a small button on the tip of the handle that opens or closes the claw itself. The claw can be used to move decorations around, remove uneaten food and retrieve any items that have been accidentally dropped into the aquarium.

NETS

Nets are available in a variety of sizes and designs. Smaller nets are generally used for catching fry and little fish. The fine webbing in these nets is soft and similar in structure to cheesecloth. Small nets are also handy for scooping out uneaten food and suspended debris from the aquarium water.

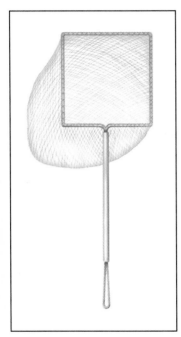

A net is handy for a variety of tasks. You'll want to purchase several nets in different sizes.

Larger nets are usually used for capturing fish. You will find that using two large nets to capture a betta is much easier than trying to do the job with only one. Your pet can easily be coaxed into the center of one net by gently nudging it with the other. You should purchase several different-sized nets so that you will be prepared to handle almost any emergency.

SCRAPERS

Scrapers are a great tool that can be used to remove unwanted algae from the aquarium glass. Most scrapers come with a two-sided head. One side has a soft sponge for wiping away loose algae. The other side of the scraper contains a tough scrub pad for removing encrusted algae and lime de-posits. Most scrapers are made of plastic and have a long handle for reaching difficult spots in the aquarium. The other end of this tool looks like a small fork and is great for turning over gravel and planting.

VACUUMS

An aquarium vacuum will help to remove unwanted debris from the water and substrate bed in your tank. You should vacuum your tank at least once a week so you can keep the water clean and crystal clear. Aquarium vacuums can be either electrically powered, battery operated or air driven. Each one of these different styles of vacuums works quite well, and it is really a matter of personal preference as to which type you purchase.

Most high-quality aquarium vacuums are designed for use along the gravel bed to suck up dirt and debris into an uplift tube. The water in the tube is filtered through a small cloth bag and then returned to the tank after it has been cleaned of suspended particles.

EXTRA EQUIPMENT FOR AQUARIUM USE

1. Scissors
2. Siphon
3. Scrub brush
4. Plastic buckets
5. Assorted sponges

TEST KITS

To keep tabs on your water conditions, you will need to have a few test kits handy. Many of these kits contain several different testers, and you can replace their fluids, strips and other measuring components as needed. You will need a pH, ammonia, nitrite and nitrate kit to monitor your water conditions when you set up your new tank. Test kits for water hardness and copper testers can be added later as you advance in the hobby.

A glass divider separates these two male bettas. Can you tell?

DIVIDERS

For years, dividers have been used to section off male bettas so that they cannot physically reach each other. Look for a divider that consists of a large plastic sheet that can be used to partition off an entire section of the aquarium. This type of divider is also useful for separating males and females in a breeding tank. Make sure that the divider has small holes in it so that water can flow through without blocking your filter's operation.

chapter 5

Plants
for the
Betta Tank

There are many good reasons for keeping live plants in the betta aquarium. (Your bettas will love you for it!) Plants aid in displaying your fish by providing an interesting and complementary background. The color, the finnage and the behavior of freshwater bettas are intensified in a naturally planted tank. Aquatic plants are also a very important part of keeping water conditions pure.

Plants have other important functions as well. They provide good shelter for pregnant females, offer shade and protect shy bettas from more aggressive tankmates. In the territorial hierarchy of any aquarium, plants can provide a safe refuge for all of your delicate and long-finned fish. Plants also help to condition the tank water by removing carbon dioxide, sulfur substances and nitrogenous wastes.

Another advantage of living plants is that they help remove deadly nitrates from the water. The biological filter on an aquarium breaks down existing ammonia into less-harmful substances, which the plants, in turn, use for food.

Purchasing Plants

Plants for the betta tank can be found at superstores and aquatic dealers. Most pet shops stock a wide variety of live plants for aquarium use. Aquatic plants are usually purchased in the form of cuttings. Plants can also be collected from ponds, but they must be carefully cleaned to avoid introducing various types of disease and such aquatic pests as snails.

By purchasing your plants from a good aquatic dealer, you can be comfortable that they are safe for your fish.

It is always best to buy your aquarium plants from a reputable dealer, just as you would your betta. Before purchasing, have a good idea of the particular types, sizes and number of plants you will need to achieve the effects that you desire.

How Many Plants Do I Need?

Avoid purchasing too many plants right away, since they tend to flourish and multiply quickly. A general rule is to allow one plant for every 6 inches squared of gravel area. If your tank is 12 inches wide and 24 inches long, begin the calculations as follows: 12 inches × 24 inches = 288 square inches of gravel. Next, you divide the total by 6:

$$\frac{288 \text{ square inches}}{6} = 48$$

For a tank that is 12 inches by 24 inches, you will need roughly 48 plants to have full coverage. Use common sense when making the final calculations because some plants are naturally "fuller" than others and will take up more space. Start with 5 to 10 plants, and then add a few more every week so that you can carefully monitor their growth and progress.

Keeping Plants Healthy
TEMPERATURE

Plants have temperature requirements just as bettas do. A large majority of pet-shop plants are tropical and need to be kept warm during the transport home.

PLANT FOODS

A variety of plant foods are available from your local aquarium dealer. Tablets and liquid feeders can be placed in the gravel near the plants' roots. Special fertilizer "plugs" can be purchased that will provide nutrition for your plants on a continuous basis. A single cutting can be placed in the center of each plug and then buried as a whole unit in the gravel.

Bringing Plants Home Safely

Plants should be kept constantly damp during the journey home. The best way is to have them bagged in water as you would if you were buying a betta.

When you arrive home, carefully lay out the plants in a pan of warm water so you can examine them more closely. If the cuttings (total plant length) are too long, trim them to the correct length with a sharp pair of scissors before you put them into your aquarium.

Lighting for Plants

The tropical plants in your aquarium should receive at least eight hours of lighting per day to ensure good health. Planted tanks generally require more intense lighting than fish-only tanks, but you can find several types of plant-grow lights at the fish shop that will work quite nicely. An ideal way to control lighting is through the use of simple timers so that peak intensity remains the same each day. As a general rule, an aquarium with water 15 inches deep should have a minimum of 60 watts (tungsten) or 20 watts (fluorescent) for each 12 inches of tank length.

Water Conditions

Clean water is very important for successful plant growth in the aquarium. Dirt and debris will settle on the surface of the leaves and clog the plant's pores.

Aquascaping

It is much easier to place plants into the aquarium after the water has been added than to try and arrange them in a dry tank. A full tank will allow you to get a better view of the final arrangement after the plants have spread out into the water. Make sure that you do not push the plants too far into the gravel. The plants' crown (the area between the plant stalk and the roots) should be just above, or at, gravel level.

SUGGESTED LIGHTING

Fluorescent

Tank Size	Watts	Hours per Day
10 gallon	15	10
15 gallon	20	10
20 gallon	20	12
30 gallon	25	12
55 gallon	30	12

Incandescent

Tank Size	Watts	Hours per Day
10 gallon	25	8
15 gallon	40	8
20 gallon	40	10
30 gallon	40	10
55 gallon	60	12

The substrate in a planted tank should consist of fine gravel or coarse sand so that water is able to move in and out of the plants' roots. Plants should be spaced far enough apart that they have room to grow, can spread their roots and have the freedom to gather sufficient light.

Floating plants should be carefully placed in the top of the tank. Plants that require attachment, such as *Microsorium pteropus,* can be carefully tied to a rock with fine fishing line to keep them stationary.

To begin aquascaping, start by putting all the tall plants near the back and sides of the aquarium. Next, fill in the center areas with short bushy plants. Taller bushy plants (such as sagittaria) can be used to hide tank corners, equipment and odd-looking spaces. Low-growing species of plants, such as acorus and micro-sorium, should be placed near the front glass.

With thoughtful placement of your plants, you can create a beautiful environment that shows your fish to their advantage.

Popular Plants for the Betta Tank

The plants described next are popular aquarium plants that will enhance your betta tank. Some require specific lighting or water conditions to thrive, but others will adapt to almost any tank.

AMAZON SWORD
(*ECHINODORUS GRANDIFLORUS*)

Amazon sword has heart-shaped leaves and is very soft. This plant requires substantial lighting.

ARROWHEAD (*SAGITTARIA GRAMINEA*)

Arrowhead requires slightly alkaline water and is very useful as a front-glass filler.

CORKSCREW TIGER VAL
(*VALLISNERIA SPIRALIS*)

Corkscrew tiger val is a beautiful plant from Southeast Asia with lighter and darker bands on the leaves. This hardy and fast-growing species thrives in all kind of water conditions and does not require intense lighting to reach its maximum growth potential. Cork-screw tiger val is a perfect plant for the betta aquarium and the beginning hobbyist.

ELODEA
(*ANACHARIS CANADENSIS*)

Elodea is a quick-growing bunched plant. This beautiful species has many green leaves coming off each stem, prefers slow currents and will thrive in almost any aquarium. Elodea is usually planted in aquarium areas that receive full lighting. This species is often used as a filler for the corners and the back of the tank.

Elodea grows quickly and adapts readily to almost any aquarium.

Foxtail is a lovely plant that's easy to keep.

FOXTAIL (*MYCROPHILLIUM HIPPUROIDES*)

The foxtail is a very hardy and fast-growing plant that needs to be pruned often. During the winter, this

Setting Up
the Aquarium

species will hit growth spurts and may clog filters if not cut back. The leaves are often golden-green under intense lighting. The foxtail is an interesting plant, but it may be difficult to acquire in some areas of the country.

AQUASCAPING TIP

When aquascaping, place plants that require more light in higher locations and use taller species to hide filters and other equipment. To create a pleasing appearance, plant similar species in groups instead of sporadically, use rocks to accent plants, and place specimens with brightly colored leaves in prominent areas.

HORNWART (*CERATOPHYLLUM DEMERSUM*)

Hornwart has stiff leaves and is very resilient to fish that attempt to munch on it.

HAIRGRASS (*ELEOCHARIS ACICULARIS*)

Hairgrass has tall, narrow leaves and requires plenty of light for growth.

Java fern will do well even without intense lighting.

JAVA FERN (*MICROSORIUM PTEROPUS*)

Java fern has large leaves that form a point at the top. It requires moderate lighting conditions.

Hygro (*Hygrophila polysperma*)

The Southeast Asian hygro is a very hardy plant. The leaves of this lovely plant grow as pairs on each side of the stem. If you provide this species with intense light, the foliage will become denser. This plant thrives in a betta aquarium and is not difficult to maintain.

Hygro is a bunch plant found in many freshwater aquariums.

Water Lettuce (*Pistia stratiotes*)

Water lettuce is a popular floating plant with long roots that provide shade and shelter for fry.

Willow Moss (*Fontinalis antipyretica*)

Willow moss has very bushy leaves and is a favorite with hobbyists.

Keeping
Your
Betta

part three

Healthy
and
Happy

chapter 6

Bringing Your
Betta
Home

Choosing the Right Dealer

Obviously, before you can bring your betta home, you need to know where to find it! When choosing a tropical fish dealer, you should consider several important factors before making any final decisions concerning shop loyalty. Visit as many local dealers as your time and budget will allow. These trips will furnish you with a solid basis for comparing the level of service, quality and maintenance of the livestock and variety of equipment.

When you visit the various shops, evaluate whether the shop's employees are friendly and offer good advice. Do they take an interest in your personal aquarium project to make sure that you find exactly what you are searching for? Is there an adequate number of personnel to provide service to you, especially during peak hours? If these criteria are met, then you have probably found a reputable and caring owner who takes pride in his or her business and in providing customer satisfaction.

Take the time to inspect all of the merchant's aquariums that display livestock. Look for signs of dealer dedication and for clues that distinguish a good shopkeeper from an uncaring merchant. A quality dealer will ensure that his or her establishment makes the best presentation possible. Are the dealer's tanks clean and well maintained? The overall condition of a dealer's tank will give you a good idea of how the fish are handled and cared for.

Upon further inspection, check to see whether the fish that are for sale are swimming without effort near the top of the tank or whether they are hiding in corners. Are the fins erect and the body properly colored and formed? Do all of the merchant's fish appear to be in good health?

When your final selection has been made, make an effort to become well acquainted with each worker in the shop. Most dealers are enthusiastic when given the opportunity to speak to repeat customers, whose tanks have over a period of time become as familiar as their own. Many caring merchants have beamed proudly at their customer's first successful betta spawning and sympathized over the loss of a hobbyist's favorite fish.

Building a personal relationship with your local dealer has many benefits. You will be provided with quality advice and the highest degree of comprehensive service available. When a merchant is familiar with your name, special interests, preferences and particular aquarium specifications, he or she is better able to help you become a successful hobbyist.

How to Pick a Healthy Betta

To start out on the right foot, it is important to make sure that the tropical fish you purchase are very healthy. When selecting new acquisitions for your home aquarium, avoid buying any "new arrivals" that your dealer has recently received from the shipper. A caring dealer will recommend that you wait until the fish have undergone a quarantine period.

Feel free to suggest to your local shopkeeper that you would like to have your new selections held for you until a reasonable quarantine period has expired.

If you notice, upon closer inspection, that there are dead fish in an apparently healthy tank, avoid buying livestock from that specific aquarium. Do not purchase "humpbacked" bettas, because this physical trait is generally an indication of old age. Dealers worth their salt (no pun intended!) will never allow a customer to purchase old or ailing fish.

When you find a fish that you like, make sure that all the fish in that tank are in good health.

New hobbyists should avoid hard-to-maintain species and unfamiliar fish. As you browse through the shop looking for tankmates for your betta, write down the names of all the fish that appeal to you.

Discuss each tankmate on the list with your dealer and ask which species are compatible with your betta, and which are hardy and do not have difficult or unique dietary requirements. More demanding species are usually better left in the expert hands of experienced hobbyists.

PHYSICAL CHARACTERISTICS

Look for the following traits when you shop:

1. Deep, rich body colors
2. No visible ulcers, boils or skin problems
3. No visible scars or wounds
4. Long and flowing, or short and erect, fins; not fins that are ragged, torn, missing, collapsed or clamped shut

Your betta should have deep color and full, extended fins.

5. Flat, smooth scales, not protruding away from the body
6. Well-rounded stomach
7. Body of normal girth, neither bloated nor emaciated
8. Visible excreta (fish waste) that should be dark, not colorless
9. Clear eyes, neither clouded over nor protruding from the sockets
10. No visible external parasites, such as ich (small white dots) or velvet (a dusty gold-colored mist)

TANK HABITS

A betta that is healthy will:

1. Swim horizontally, with its head neither elevated nor lowered

2. Swim without effort

3. Swim throughout the entire length of the aquarium, not lurking in corners or hiding behind decorations

4. Breathe normally, not heave rapidly or gulp for air

If the apparent health of the fish does not meet these criteria, it is better to exercise a little patience and wait for healthier specimens to arrive before making a purchase.

Stocking Limits

Before you purchase any livestock for your new aquarium, it is essential to calculate the total number of fish (your betta and its tankmates) that can be safely housed in your tank. The maximum number of fish that can be kept safely within your aquarium tank is known as the *carrying capacity*.

Overstocking is probably the most common error made by beginning hobbyists. You must be consciously aware of your aquarium's carrying capacity. The old rule of thumb, "one inch of fish per gallon," has serious limitations. For example, a 2-inch kissing gourami *(Helostoma temmincki)* will take up much more water volume and produce a lot more waste than a 2-inch pencil fish *(Nannostomus aripirangensis)*.

The following mathematical formula will give you a good idea of the total amount of average-sized fish that can be safely maintained in each of your aquariums. This formula uses a more realistic standard rule (3 inches of fish per square foot of filter bed).

Tank width: 12 inches

Tank length: 30 inches

> **THE QUALITIES OF A GOOD DEALER**
>
> A good tropical fish dealer will greet you pleasantly and will always ask you if help is needed. Good dealers will also help you understand equipment and aquarium basics, disclose the pros and cons of your selections, refuse to sell you fish that are not compatible, and have clean display tanks containing healthy fish.

First, you must multiply the tank width by the tank length:

12 inches (1 foot) × 30 inches (2.5 feet) = 2.5 square feet.

Next, multiply the result (2.5) by 3:

2.5 square feet × 3 inches of fish = 7.5 inches.

So, an aquarium measuring 12 inches by 30 inches can safely keep fish whose total combined length adds up to 7.5 inches.

If you are stocking larger tankmates such as the blue gourami *(Trichogaster trichopterus)*, you need to double the final figure for safety. Once again, a little common sense can make a substantial difference in the success or failure of your aquarium.

Fish store dealers generally bend the rules for stocking limits because of higher turnover rates in their display tanks. Please do not make the mistake of using their poor example in your own home aquarium. Be sure to provide adequate space for each fish so that your new pets will not suffer from oxygen starvation and be stressed out before they have even had a chance to become acclimated to their new home.

Use common sense in stocking your tank—if you are including larger fish, such as a blue gourami, err on the side of fewer fish.

New Tank Syndrome

"New tank syndrome" is a problem that can occur during the period when your new aquarium is maturing. If the ammonia or nitrite levels in your aquarium become too high and are not being properly converted to less harmful substances (nitrates) through normal bacterial action, the result may be physical ailments or the death of your new aquatic pets.

75

Fish that are suffering from the ill effects of new tank syndrome will often be pale in color, have clamped fins, hang near the bottom of the tank and hide behind decorations. If you notice any unusual behaviors after adding new fish to your aquarium, test the ammonia and nitrite levels of your water immediately.

On occasion, new tank syndrome will strike very quickly and without warning. It is not unusual for newly purchased fish in an aquarium to look perfectly normal at night when the lights are turned off, only to be found dead the following morning.

To be safe, wait until a few weeks have passed and then add one or two small fish per week to the aquarium. This gradual increase in livestock will keep any additional ammonia levels within a minimum range.

Remember, it is vital that you continually check your water conditions (ammonia, nitrites, nitrates and pH) as the system matures. Frequent water changes (5 percent per day) will help to lower any excess levels of waste buildup.

A cloudiness will appear in the water during the first week of cycling. Don't panic! Cloudiness is a sign that beneficial bacterial are in bloom, which is perfectly normal. With proper filtration, the water should become clear again within a few days.

Transportation Home

Once you have made the commitment to purchase a betta, you must take responsible action to make sure that your new aquatic friends have the best possible chance of survival. When your betta is being moved from a dealer's tank to your home aquarium, it is important to minimize the shock of transport.

One of the most important aspects of your betta's health is the way that it is physically handled during transport. All efforts should be made on the part of the dealer and hobbyist to make sure that the betta and its tankmates are packed properly for travel. For example, just a little bit of extra water in the bag can reduce stress greatly and make all the difference in the world.

I firmly believe that all fish should be double bagged to avoid puncture and leaks. For example, if a catfish (in a panic) should happen to rupture the first bag, the second bag provides another layer of plastic to slow down water loss. It is always possible that a shipping bag can be flawed or contain a small pinhole that will leak during your trip. Using double bags as a safety measure is just good common sense.

The shipping bags should be dark in color to help calm your betta and its tankmates during transport. If none are available, you can add a few drops of blue food coloring to the water to simulate the effects of darkness, or wrap a thin dark cloth around each bag.

> **BETTA TRANSPORTATION TIPS**
>
> 1. Ask the dealer if he or she can add pure oxygen to the fish's bag.
>
> 2. Don't run errands after buying your fish—bring it directly home.
>
> 3. Turn the bag upside down in the carrier so there are no corners.
>
> 4. Keep your vehicle cool, because hot fish consume more oxygen.

The shipping container itself should be well insulated. Appropriate packing material such as Styrofoam peanuts can be used to absorb shocks and prevent heat loss from occurring during cold weather conditions.

Acclimation

Maintaining a simple quarantine tank may not be fun, but it is truly the best way to get your hobby off to a good start. Through the diligent practice of quarantining, you can avoid outbreaks of disease—and the addition of countless varieties of medications that can create havoc in a display tank. Purchase the proper equipment necessary to set up a quarantine tank if you do not already have one.

After quarantining, you will finally be ready to introduce your new aquatic pets into their aquarium. Exercise a little patience when you add your fish. First,

*Keep the lights
low when intro-
ducing a new
fish into the tank.
The darkness is
soothing to the
new resident.*

turn off all aquarium lights so that your new arrivals will not be molested by previous tank residents (if there are any). The comforting darkness will also help to reduce stress.

It is likely that the temperature of the water in your fish's bag will be different from that of the water in the tank. Sudden changes in temperature can quickly cause stress. Float the bag in the aquarium for 15 minutes as you slowly add tank water to it. This will help to equalize the temperatures between the two environments. After equalization, carefully tip the bag forward and allow your new fish to swim out on its own.

NEW FISH TIP

Before adding new fish to your tank, rearrange a few of the tank decorations and then turn off all aquarium lights. After release, watch the tank carefully for at least an hour while the new inhabitants become accustomed to their surroundings and other tankmates.

By planning ahead, your betta and its tankmates will continually receive excellent care and live long, happy lives.

chapter 7

Feeding
Your Betta

Even as a beginning hobbyist, you probably already know the basics about feeding tropical fish. However, the feeding of tropical fish can easily be an art in itself. There are now so many natural and prepared foods on the market from which to choose

that new aquarium keepers can quickly become confused about nutritional issues.

If you want your betta and its tankmates to grow strong and healthy and show good coloration, you will need to give them a proper diet. Good nutrition is really not as confusing as you might think. Most commercial foods provide the majority of nutrients that your fish will require for good health. Periodically providing other treats, such as live and frozen foods, will give your pets the extra energy and vitality that they need.

79

In the wild, bettas feed mainly on insects that fall into the water in which they live. In the home aquarium, the proteins, fats, vitamins, fiber and carbohydrates that are normally obtained in their natural diet must be provided by you. Proteins and fats provide energy, minerals are important in bone formation and fluid regulation, fiber helps to prevent gastric disorders, and vitamins aid in keeping the body tissues resilient to disease. A well-fed betta will be less likely to contract a disease than a poorly fed one.

Bettas need to be fed frequent, small meals because they have a rapid metabolic rate. In an overly clean aquarium system, there may not be adequate amounts of natural foods, such as algae, that would normally provide your bettas with a little something to tide them over until the next scheduled feeding. The daily meals that you supply may be the only source of food that your betta receives.

A Betta's Nutritional Needs

To understand the basics involved in feeding, you must first be aware of the various types of nutritional foods available to betta owners. With a simple knowledge of fundamental nutritional principles, you will quickly gain a better understanding of how to properly feed your betta.

There are many good nutritional sources that can be combined to form a proper diet for your betta. These include brine shrimp, dry flake food, fresh shrimp, algae, daphnae, tubifex worms and beef heart. These are all good sources of nutrition if given in proper amounts.

VITAMINS

Vitamins are a vital part of a betta's diet, and will combat eye problems, skin hemorrhages and anemia. Feeding your bettas a wide variety of foods that contain vitamins will help eliminate the risk of certain diseases and will also fulfill a large part of their dietary needs.

PROTEINS

Proteins help your betta build strong muscle and body tissue. These can be provided by feeding your betta small bits of meat, fish, insects and plenty of premanufactured foods. Proteins, which are built from amino acids, are needed to promote growth. It is important to remember that younger fish and fry will need a little more protein in their diet than their adult counterparts.

A diet rich in vitamins from a variety of foods will help to keep your betta healthy.

CARBOHYDRATES

Carbohydrates provide energy for your betta and help it resist disease, but they may be harmful in excessive levels. Carbohydrate-based foods should be given minimally.

MINERALS

Minerals are very important to your betta's health and can be supplied in liquid form or through frequent water changes.

Feeding Schedule

It is much better to feed your betta three or four small meals per day instead of one large serving. Smaller fish and fry should be fed even more often to ensure proper growth. A general rule is to feed only the amount that all of the fish in your aquarium can eat in a period of three to five minutes. Fast your fish one day a week; this helps to keep their dietary tract in good working condition.

There are many sociable bettas and other tankmates who will literally beg for food by swimming up to the glass and imitating a starving animal. Avoid the temptation to toss in a pinch of food every time these moochers look hungry or distressed; you will only overfeed them. If you are keeping nocturnal species along with your betta, be sure to feed at night as well as during the day, so that all tank residents obtain proper nutrition.

Bettas are not aggressive feeders and will often hang back while other fish greedily devour every bit of food that is put into the aquarium. If your betta has other tankmates, you need to carefully watch the overall social situation at feeding time. If aggressive fish are frequently squeezing out your betta at mealtime, either add a little more food at each feeding or use a parti-tion so that your betta can eat in privacy. Fortunately, these remedies are not required in most community situations.

HIGH-PROTEIN FOODS TO SUPPLEMENT YOUR BETTA'S DIET

1. Red meat
2. White meat
3. Fish
4. Insects
5. Worms

A Varied Diet

Vary your betta's diet so that it does not become bored with eating the same foods day after day. Think about it. Would you like to eat meat loaf every day for a year? Bettas have been known to stop feeding entirely when they have been offered only one type of food for a long period of time.

PREPACKAGED FOODS

Manufacturers offer a wide variety of well-balanced processed foods that are easy to feed and store. Small tablet foods can be softened with water and then stuck to the aquarium glass at different levels in the tank or dropped to the bottom; this ensures that all the fishes at different feeding levels will get the nutrition they need.

FLAKE FOODS

Flake foods are a good staple for your betta and its tankmates. Initially, flakes will float at the water's surface and then sink later on as they become saturated. Flaked vegetable matter, such as spirulina, contains high levels of betacarotene, is easy to digest, contains stabilized vitamin C and does not cloud the aquarium water. This product also offers a combination of fish meal, wheat flour, shrimp meal, fish protein, egg, oil and multivitamin supplements.

Commercial fish food is available in a variety of forms—flakes are especially good for bettas.

Many standard flake foods contain a large number of different ingredients. The average hobbyist would be hard-pressed to provide a diet as complete as that found in good quality flake foods. When selecting flake foods, look for those that contain a moisture level that is less than 4 percent of the total product. Many nutrients will dissipate quickly from food with a high moisture content when the food is placed in the aquarium water.

PELLET FOODS

Pellet foods are designed to either float or sink. Floating pellets provide good nutrition for surface feeders but are generally too large and coarse for your betta to consume. Sinking pellets can be gobbled up by mid-level and bottom feeders as the pellets sink, and are generally used for species such as goldfish and large cichlids. Granular foods sink quickly and are perfect for any bottom-dwelling inhabitants, such as catfish, that share your betta's home.

Frozen Foods

Frozen foods are available in a wide variety and mixture of different vegetable and animal products. Many contain only vegetables; others may use a variety of meats and animal protein as the main ingredients. By mixing and matching frozen foods, you will be able to supply your betta with many interesting and nutritional meals.

It is important to keep frozen food chilled until you are ready to feed. Foods such as brine shrimp will spoil quickly, and spoiled food will pollute your tank. Never refreeze any frozen foods after they have thawed. Refreezing strips the food of most of its nutrients.

Freeze-Dried Foods

Freeze-dried foods contain no moisture and can be stored away for long periods of time. Most of the standard frozen foods are also available in freeze-dried form, and will stay fresh as long as they are stored in an area free from excessive heat and moisture.

Liquid Foods

There are many types of liquid foods available, but they are usually used to feed young fry. Liquid food should been avoided for adult fish, because it tends to quickly foul the tank as it spreads through the water and is left uneaten.

FEEDER INSECTS

Many insects such as earthworms, grasshoppers, caterpillars, wingless flies and wood lice can be cleaned and diced up for an occasional treat that your betta will really love.

Live Food

Despite the fact that they are in a captive environment, bettas still enjoy hunting live food when it is provided. However, you must take precautions when using live foods because there is a high risk of transmitting disease into the tank. If you collect live foods from clean ponds, rivers, streams or gardens, always rinse them with clear water before use. Take care to remove any uneaten food immediately to avoid fouling the water.

Your bettas will enjoy *rotifers*, which are small inverte-
brates that can be obtained from rotifer farms, frequently found in coastal states such as Florida.
Earthworms, white worms and red worms are readily
accepted by most bettas, but once again note the caution about disease. Live brine shrimp are available at
most pet stores, or can be easily cultured in pickle jars
at home.

*Bettas will enjoy
the occasional
earthworm, but be
sure to rinse well
before feeding.*

Around the House

Small quantities of household foods can be periodically added to your betta's diet. Thes include peas, sliv-
ers of lean meat, lettuce, potato, shellfish, spinach and
cheese. Brine shrimp and worms can also be cultured
at home to provide a constant supply of live food that
is disease free. Do not overuse household foods such as
meat and vegetables. Your betta's digestive system is
not as complex as yours, and will not tolerate the large
amounts and types of food that are normally reserved
for human consumption.

Vegetables

Vegetables are an important aspect of a betta's well-
rounded diet. You can offer your betta a small piece of
lettuce or a little bit of cooked spinach. Shelled,
cooked peas have always been a favorite treat for my
own bettas. Remember that all fresh vegetables should

be thoroughly rinsed before they are added to your
aquarium. Many vegetables are sprayed with insect
repellents that can be dangerous to your betta's health
if they are not removed.

Lettuce can be held at the top of the tank with an
aquarium clip. Having the lettuce at the top lets your
betta graze without much interference from mid- and
bottom-dwelling species. The clip will also keep the
vegetables from falling to the bottom or clogging filter
inlets. Remove the lettuce each day so that a fresh
piece can be added.

ALGAE

Research has shown that green algae benefits tropical
fish by providing them with the vitamins and nutrients
needed for good health and outstanding color.

*Algae growing on
rocks and leaves
will be a natural
supplement to
your fish's diet.*

Good plant-lighting spectrums, such as that provided
by actinic blue bulbs, can be invaluable in the process
of algae growth. Excess algae, which will inevitably
form on the glass, can be quickly and easily removed
with an algae scraper. Algae that has grown on top of
rocks and plant leaves can be left there for your aquatic pets to graze upon. After the algae has grown into a
healthy "crop," you will notice that all your fish will
continually feed upon this natural food, and it in turn
will prolong their lives and bolster their health.

When insufficient light is present, brown algae may grow in abundance. As the aquarium ages, or more of the proper spectrum of lighting is added, this algae may change into a green form, which will be greatly appreciated by your bettas and their tankmates.

GROWING YOUR OWN ALGAE

Many aquarists who prefer a clean-looking tank culture their own algae in small tanks or jars. A simple method to ensure a continual supply for feeding purposes is to put a single piece of rock in a small tank or jar filled with water and then place it near a window that receives plenty of natural sunlight. After algae growth is complete and the rock is covered, it can then be placed in the main tank for your fish to nibble on. Another piece of rock can then be put into the tank by the window to start the process anew.

If you use this practical home-culture method, you will have a constant supply of algae for feeding, without the hassle of unsightly overgrowth in the main display tank. Water in the growth tank should be replaced periodically after three or four algae growth cycles have been completed.

Overfeeding

One of the main rules of aquatic nutrition is don't overfeed. Your betta's stomach is not much larger than the size of its eye. It does not take vast amounts of food to keep your pet full. Continual overfeeding will cause the water in your tank to foul, which in turn can lead to disease and other health problems. To help avoid the temptation to overfeed, simply use premeasured portions that have been separated in plastic bags. Vacuuming your tank once a week and frequent water changes will minimize any fouling of water.

Appetite Loss

Even if you provide the proper foods, incidents will still arise when your betta simply stops eating. But what causes this sudden lack of appetite? Incorrect pH levels, polluted water, poor health, disease and other improper aquarium conditions will all affect your betta's feeding habits.

Make sure that you check the pH, temperature and nitrate levels if your fish suddenly stops feeding. Overcrowding will cause many fish to become stressed and will encourage them to fast. Diseased fish will also stop eating regularly as they become sicker and sicker.

Evaluate your tank conditions if your betta stops eating. Is the water chemistry balanced properly? Are there too many fish in the tank?

By providing good aquarium conditions and proper diet, your fish will live longer and healthier lives. A "fishy buffet" may be just the thing your own bettas need to improve their health and vitality.

chapter 8

Healthy Tank, Healthy Fish

As a caring and conscientious tropical fishkeeper, you have the moral responsibility to do the very best that you can for your "wet pets." After all, your bettas and other fish will give you years of enjoyment and relaxation. They have other benefits as well. Researchers

have found that people who keep aquarium fish in their home or office are less stressed physically and emotionally, and live longer lives than those who do not. Aquarium fish can also be a great educational tool for learning about the natural world. Because your tropical fish help you live a healthier life, you should return the favor by keeping them in prime condition through the use of good disease prevention techniques.

Stress, poor diet, incorrect water conditions and incompatible tank-mates are just a few of the factors that can increase the chances of disease striking. Through diligent maintenance routines and procedures, any hobbyist can improve existing aquarium conditions, or stay one step ahead of disease problems when setting up a new system. It takes only a few minutes a day to ensure success.

Maintaining a Healthy Tank

There are no real secrets to keeping your betta happy and healthy. All you need to do is follow a few simple rules and keep a sharp eye out for any disease that may occur. It is important to check your betta's health at the same time that you check the aquarium conditions each and every day. If you constantly keep abreast of the conditions in your tank, you will be able to quickly correct any problems that may manifest themselves.

DAILY

It is vital that all mechanical equipment is functioning properly on a daily basis. Are the filter systems putting out the optimal flow the manufacturer suggests?

Checking the water temperature is another important daily routine. Any fluctuation in temperature of more than 2° from the norm can quickly cause a health problem. If the temperature is not correct, check to make sure that your heater is not stuck on or off. Replace faulty heaters immediately; if possible, install a heater containing an internal regulator.

An excess of natural or artificial lighting may also be the cause of overheating. You may need to check the amount of natural sunlight that the tank receives every day, and check the overall duration and intensity of the artificial lighting if the temperature is moving into a higher than normal range.

Check the air pumps in the aquarium to make sure they are in good working condition. If the pumps are not putting out the correct amount of air, they can usually be rebuilt by replacing worn diaphragms with packaged rebuild parts; these parts can be found at your local fish shop or special ordered for you.

Every morning, take a quick inventory of all the fish that you have in your tank. If any are dead, remove them immediately. If any seem to be ill, transfer them to a hospital tank and begin treatment immediately. If you check the health of your fish daily, you will keep diseases from spreading to other individuals.

WEEKLY

I recommend that you perform at least a 15-percent water change in each of your aquarium tanks every week. Even in the betta's natural environment, the water is constantly being cleansed and replaced through rains, tidal flow and other natural causes. Stop for a moment and pretend that the water in your aquarium is your own personal water supply for the day. Would you feel comfortable drinking it? Remember, your betta has to *live* in it.

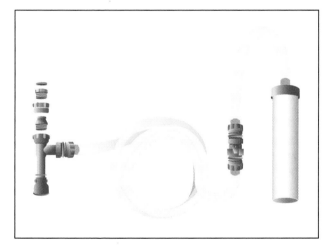

A water changer can be used to siphon and refill the tank while maintaining acceptable water conditions.

Every week, siphon off any debris that has accumulated on the substrate's surface area. Check your pH and nitrate levels to make sure that they are within the proper range required by your betta. If not, you can modify the pH in slow intervals through the use of chemical additions.

If the nitrate levels are too high, the best remedy is to do daily water changes of 20 percent until the levels return to normal. Check your aquarium conditions so that you can identify and correct any problem that is causing the nitrate levels to rise, such as poor filtration, overfeeding or overcrowding.

Clean excess algae growth from the glass surfaces. An excessive overgrowth of algae can cause the oxygen levels in the aquarium to drop. This lower oxygen level will stress your fish and could cause medical problems.

Remove excess algae from the glass with a scraper.

MONTHLY

Clean all filter pads and other mediums by rinsing them under clean tap water. Do not use scalding or boiling water for this task, because the extreme heat will destroy beneficial bacteria. Remember to soak filter mediums in a solution of dechlorinator for a few minutes before returning them to their units; this ensures that there is no residual chlorine left from the tap water. Even a small amount of chlorine can kill your betta.

Quarantine Tanks

After bringing your new betta home, place it in a quarantine tank for a period of two weeks (unless it is being used as a starter fish). Placing your new acquisition in a small holding tank with water conditions that are the same as those in the betta's permanent aquarium will give you time to see if any latent diseases or physical problems exist.

Bettas undergo a tremendous amount of stress during shipping from a wholesaler's outlet to your local dealer's shop. A quarantine tank will provide your betta with a suitable transportation recovery period and allow it to regain its strength before it is placed in its new home.

Examining Your Fish

Each day, you should carefully check the health of your fish. Look closely at your betta's physical condition. Is your betta swimming normally, or is it consistently lurking in the corners of the tank? Are its eyes bright and alert, or clouded over? Are your betta's fins erect, or clamped shut and drooping? Is its spine straight or curved? Does the body have normal, well-rounded proportions, or is the stomach swollen or sunken?

The importance of a regular observation routine cannot be overemphasized. Any clamped fins, shimmying, loss of appetite, paling or darkening of colors, increased respiration or other abnormal behavior is a warning sign that disease or environmental conditions may have taken a turn for the worse.

KNOW YOUR BETTA'S HABITS

Part of being a good fishkeeper is learning how to recognize unnatural behaviors. If your betta is acting strangely, chances are that there is a problem somewhere in your aquarium. Being able to identify odd behavior is the first step in disease prevention. The following list of abnormal betta behaviors will alert you to a potential problem:

1. Scratching itself on tank decorations or gravel
2. Normally active but now moving slowly or not at all
3. Floating upside down or swimming sideways
4. Floating to the top or struggling to rise from the gravel
5. A bloated look
6. Refusing to eat
7. Visible damage to its fins, eyes or scales
8. Spots or patches that you have never seen before
9. Hanging around the heater all day
10. Fins continuously clamped shut

If you notice any of these problems, check your aquarium conditions immediately.

Stress and Other Factors

Most illnesses found in aquarium fish are the direct result of stress caused by poor environmental conditions outside of the body. Pathogenic problems (those that are not environmentally induced) are usually dormant until the betta has become weakened by fluctuating environmental factors. In the home aquarium, your betta lives in an enclosed ecosystem that is very vulnerable to imbalance compared with the natural stability of its native environment.

Observe your fish. If your betta is not swimming normally or has another change in its behavior, it may be ill.

When you first notice the warning signs that an illness is present in your aquarium, don't panic. Sit back for a moment and carefully observe the efficiency of the equipment, the water conditions and other stress-related factors. Once you have analyzed all of this information, you will be able to make a sound judgment regarding the proper course of action to be taken.

Common Illnesses

The following list of common illnesses will give you general guidelines for identifying and treating disease. Keep in mind that several types of common medications and salt treatments may be detrimental to living plants, some species of catfish, and other tropical fish. Check the manufacturer's warnings on the label carefully if you are treating any fish without a quarantine tank.

FUNGUS

Occurrence: Very common.

Symptoms: White growths on the body that are fluffy in appearance. These growths can also be found on the fin areas.

Cause: The fungus attacks regions where the mucus or slime coating on the fish has worn off because of damage by parasites or injury. Fungus is generally the *Saprolegnia* and *Achlya* species.

Treatment: Spot treat with gentian violet or methylene blue; use aquarium fungicide in extreme cases.

MOUTH FUNGUS

Occurrence: Infrequent.

Symptoms: Cotton-like growths around the mouth or patchy-white skin.

Cause: Usually *Saprolegnia* species, occurring after other infection has set in.

Treatment: Commercial fungus treatment or methylene blue. If these treatments are not effective, consult your veterinarian about antibiotics.

INTESTINAL PARASITES

Occurrence: Infrequent.

Symptoms: Worms showing through the vent; emaciation.

Causes: Different varieties of intestinal worms.

Treatment: Standard fungus cure or veterinarian-prescribed anthelminthic given in the diet. Add 1 tablespoon of aquarium salt for each 5 gallons of water to

---

A QUICK REFERENCE GUIDE TO DISEASE

The following table of symptoms and possible causes will give you a quick reference guide for trouble-shooting disease problems. Remember, a single symptom can be indicative of many different types of diseases. This table will provide you with a general pathway toward locating the correct problem.

SYMPTOM	POSSIBLE PROBLEM
Spots on skin	Ich, velvet
Slimy skin	Parasites
Cotton-like growths	Fungus
Parasite visible	Anchor worm, fish lice
Ulcer visible	Bacteria
Faded color	Stress
Bad equilibrium	Swim bladder disorder
Rapid breathing	Low oxygen, gill flukes
Erratic behavior	Poor water conditions
Convulsions	Poison
Constant scratching	Flukes, ich
Weight loss	Stress, tuberculosis

help with osmoregulation. Remove any activated carbon. Change 10 percent of the water daily.

Swim Bladder Disease

Occurrence: Infrequent.

Symptoms: Abnormal swimming patterns or loss of balance.

Causes: Bacterial infection, physical injury to swim bladder from fighting or during transportation from dealer, poor water quality.

Treatment: Treat with an antibiotic in a clean, shallow tank. Change the water frequently.

If fins are injured while fighting, fin rot can develop. These two male bettas could do some real damage if they were not separated by a glass divider.

Fin Rot

Occurrence: Very common.

Symptoms: Inflamed rays; torn, ragged or disintegrating fins.

Causes: Either poor water quality or fin injury is the main cause of this disease, a highly contagious bacterial infection that can completely erode the fins and tail all the way down to the body. Fin rot is frequently followed by a secondary fungal infection.

Treatment: Spot treat infected areas with gentian violet. Add 1 tablespoon of aquarium salt for each 5 gallons of water to help with osmoregulation. Remove activated carbon from all filters during the treatment period.

Frequent water changes are necessary to help improve your betta's condition.

POP EYE

Occurrence: Infrequent.

Symptoms: Inflamed eyes protruding from their sockets. Often the eyes will develop a haze that is white in color. Inflamed eye sockets are also common.

Causes: Parasites or poor environmental conditions.

Treatment: The only thing that you can do to help your betta overcome pop eye is to improve the aquarium's water conditions with frequent changes, and add 1 tablespoon of aquarium salt per 5 gallons of water to help with osmoregulation. Check water conditions with test kits to ensure that they remain within the correct range.

VELVET

Occurrence: Very common.

Symptoms: A golden-velvet or gray-colored coating on the body or fin areas. Your betta will look like it has been sprinkled with gold dust.

Cause: *Oodinium* parasite. The adult parasites will attach themselves to your betta and then fall off after a period of about one week. These parasites will sink down into the gravel and begin to multiply. The new parasites are then released into the water and will reinfect the fish in your aquarium. If the parasites cannot find a living host within a period of about three days, they will die.

Treatment: Commercial malachite green remedy. Add 1 tablespoon of aquarium salt for each 5 gallons of water.

ICH

Occurrence: Very common.

Symptoms: The appearance, on the body or fins, of small white spots that resemble little grains of salt. Fish that are infected with ich will scratch themselves on gravel and decorations during the advanced stages of this disease.

Cause: *Ichthyopthirius* parasite. Adult parasites will fall off the host, sink to the bottom of the tank, and multiply in the gravel. New parasites will be released to find another host.

Treatment: Commercial ich remedy (formalin or malachite green). If the afflicted betta is removed to a quarantine tank, the main aquarium's water must still be treated to kill off the remaining free-swimming parasites.

Even if a fish with ich is placed in a hospital tank, the main aquarium must also be treated to eradicate the parasite.

BACTERIAL SEPTICEMIA

Occurrence: Infrequent.

Symptoms: Blood streaks appear on the fins and body. Other symptoms include hemorrhages, listlessness and refusal to eat. This disease usually occurs after a fish has been afflicted with fin rot or skin infections.

Causes: *Pseudomonas* or *Streptococcus* bacteria.

Treatment: Antibacterial Furan2 or Triple Sulfa. Change the water every 24 hours.

TUBERCULOSIS

Occurrence: Infrequent.

Symptoms: Dull-colored body, clamped fins, weight loss, ulcers, and pop eye in some cases.

Cause: Bacterial disease that is highly contagious. *WARNING!* This disease can be transferred to humans through contact with the infected areas.

Treatment: There is really no effective treatment of this disease, and in my opinion it is *not worth risking your own health* in order to try any remedy. Strict care must be used when handling infected animals! Plastic gloves are recommended when removing the infected betta from the aquarium. A betta that has this disease should be euthanized IMMEDIATELY. Do not leave the infected fish in the tank, because other tankmates will eat it and can develop the disease shortly after.

Fish Lice

Occurrence: Infrequent.

Symptoms: Disk-shaped parasites can be found attached to the skin of the betta. Ulcers can be sighted near the point of parasitic attachment. Bacterial or fungus problems may follow.

Cause: Crustacean parasite. After feeding on the skin, the adult parasite will leave its host and lay gelatin-like capsules full of eggs. Often the eggs will not hatch until the temperature rises, and may stay in the tank for long periods of time.

> ### MAINTAINING YOUR BETTA'S COAT
>
> The betta's slime coat has a very important function in preventing the loss of salts from the gills and skin. If large areas of the slime coat are worn off, these salts will be lost from your betta's body. This loss can lead to a higher risk of disease and heart failure.
>
> Stress coat (which contains aloe vera) will help heal tissue that has been damaged by the loss of slime coating, and will protect your betta against disease. I recommend the use of this product when adding any new fish to your tank, or during any transportation procedure that requires the use of a net.

Treatment: Remove the parasite from the betta with a small pair of tweezers. Dab any wounds using a cotton swab that has been dipped in Mercurochrome. Remove water from the main tank and sterilize all decorations and gravel. Unfortunately, the only real way to correct this disease problem is to start over with your system.

Gill Parasites

Occurrence: Infrequent.

Symptoms: Labored respiration, scratching, glazed eyes and loss of motor control.

Cause: Flukes (*Dactylogyrus*).

Treatment: Sterazin.

SLIME DISEASE

Occurrence: Very common.

Symptoms: A gray coating on the body or fins, scratching, frayed fins and shimmying.

Causes: *Costia, Cyclochaeta* or *Chilodonella* parasites.

Treatment: Commercial remedy of malachite green and frequent water changes. Short-term formalin and salt baths will help as well.

DROPSY

Occurrence: Very infrequent.

Symptoms: Swollen body, protruding scales, bloated eyes.

Cause: Organ failure from cancer or poor environmental conditions.

Treatment: Antibacterial should be given through medicated food. Improvement of water quality through water changes will help to clear up this disease. Full recovery from dropsy is rare.

CONSTIPATION

Occurrence: Very common.

Symptoms: Poor appetite, swollen stomach region, inactivity.

Cause: Incorrect diet, overfeeding.

Treatment: Fast your betta for several days. Add ½ teaspoon of magnesium per gallon. Change your betta's diet to live foods for several weeks.

Other Causes of Disease

POISONING

To avoid inadvertently poisoning your betta, never allow any materials constructed of metal to come into contact with the aquarium water. Metal hoods and equipment clips are two potential sources of danger. Use plastic clips and make sure that the glass cover on your aquarium fits correctly so that no water comes into contact with the hood and light fixture.

Another common source of water poisoning in aquariums is household cleaning, cosmetic and insect-control products. Never use insecticides, hair sprays or mist cleaners in the same vicinity as your aquarium.

IMPROPER DIET AND OVERFEEDING

A balanced diet that consists of a wide variety of commercially packaged flakes, small servings of fresh lettuce and peas, and live foods such as water fleas (Daphnia) and tubifex worms will go far to keep your betta healthy.

Overfeeding your betta on a regular basis will cause poor water conditions in your tank. Premeasure each serving of food so that you are not tempted to add too much.

FRIGHTENING YOUR FISHES

Sudden changes in lighting (switching on the aquarium lights while the room itself is still dark) can cause your betta to panic and injure itself on decorations and tank walls as it makes a mad dash for cover. Physical damage to scales and fins will open the door for bacteria to attack. To avoid this unfortunate situation, gradually increase room lighting by opening drapes and turning on lamps before you switch on the aquarium lights.

In addition, if you constantly alter tank decorations and stick your hands into the aquarium water, your betta will become stressed and will be at a higher risk for disease.

Hospital Tanks

A hospital tank can be set up at very little cost. Begin with a small tank (5 to 10 gallons) and a sponge filter or other filtration system that does not contain carbon.

(Carbon tends to absorb medication and reduce its efficacy.) Frequent water changes that are needed during the treatment of a sick betta will also be much easier to carry out in a small hospital tank.

A good quality heater will allow you to monitor and fluctuate water temperatures as needed. Diseases such as ich can be treated much faster by raising the standard temperature by a few degrees.

Don't frighten your betta with sudden changes in lighting. A "panic attack" can cause your fish to swim wildly into the tank décor, damaging those gorgeous fins.

KEEP SEPARATE NETS FOR GOOD HEALTH

When working with diseased fish, never use the net from the hospital tank to transport fish back into the main aquarium. All nets that are involved in the transport of ill fish should be sterilized with hot water before and after use to keep disease from spreading.

Another way to ensure successful medical treatment is to keep the hospital lights dim. Several types of medications can have their effectiveness reduced by bright lighting. Add a few extra airstones to the hospital tank to increase oxygen supply, since many forms of medication tend to reduce the oxygen supply in the aquarium.

The water conditions in the hospital tank should be similar to the parameters of the main tank from which the infected betta was taken. This will help to reduce stress caused by moving the afflicted betta to a new environment.

One way to make your sick betta feel more secure after it has been placed in the treatment ward is to decorate its hospital tank with a small amount of gravel and a few artificial plants. (Many live plants can be destroyed by medications.) An "at home" feeling will reduce stress and increase the odds of successful treatment.

Using a hospital tank for an ailing betta is much better than treating your fish in its display tank. The separate tank lowers the risk of the disease spreading to other fish in the same aquarium.

Moreover, treatment with antibiotics and other medications will always destroy part of the aquarium's essential bacteria and reduce the efficiency of the main tank's biological filtration system. These conditions can lead to even greater health problems and outbreaks of new diseases. A hospital tank will prevent that problem.

Before and after each use, the hospital tank and all of its equipment should be thoroughly sterilized with hot water to make sure that all unwanted organisms are destroyed. Transfer a sick betta in a plastic bag or large cup. A fishnet can be easily contaminated with disease.

Treatment Tips

Avoid the temptation to run down to the local merchant to purchase several different types of medications in the hopes that you will catch the right disease by process of elimination. A chronic overdose of medications will kill your betta just as quickly as if you did nothing at all.

If you have checked all available resources and have not been able to identify the disease or its cause, get the assistance of a professional. A local vet or fish dealer may be able to give you the expert advice that you will need to take care of the problem.

When medication is required, follow all the instructions on the package to the letter. Avoid the temptation of adding extra medication just to be on the safe side. There are good reasons why manufacturers put specific directions and dosage amounts on the bottle or carton. Don't second-guess them.

Make sure that you carry through the process of administering medication for the entire suggested time of treatment. Don't stop medicating simply because your betta begins to look healthy again. After a few days of treatment, you may have destroyed the active pathogens but not wiped out any new offspring that are still waiting to hatch.

Just because your fish appears to be on the mend does not mean you should discontinue medication. Follow the directions of the manufacturer.

The Old-Fashioned Salt Bath

One of the oldest remedies for treating such diseases as ich and fungus is a saltwater bath. I have used this method for over 25 years and have found that it has a high rate of success in treating various diseases.

Simply add 1 teaspoon of table salt for each gallon of water in your hospital tank. Keeping adding 1 teaspoon of salt twice a day for the first five days. If the infected betta is not completely well by the fifth day, continue to add 1 teaspoon of salt for another three days.

The Medicine Chest

There are a few items that you should keep on hand for periodic use. Collect all of the following items for your own "doctor's kit."

One package of antibiotics

One copper-based medication for parasite problems

One pair of rubber gloves for handling fish and medications

One bottle of malachite green

One small box of marine salt

One complete pH test kit

One complete nitrite/nitrate test kit

One complete ammonia test kit

One bottle of dechlorinator

One bottle of methylene blue

Cotton swabs

Bleach to disinfect equipment

One bottle of Mercurochrome

One pair of scissors

One pair of tweezers

One magnifying glass

One clean hand towel

Destroying a Fish Humanely

If your fish becomes incurably ill, euthanasia is the correct procedure to take. If your betta cannot function properly, it is inhumane to allow it to continue living in a poor physical condition. The quickest way to destroy a betta is to place it in a plastic bag full of aquarium water, and put it in the freezer. Your betta will simply "go to sleep" in a painless fashion.

With proper aquarium management procedures in place, you should not have to destroy your fish. A few maintenance routines, a careful eye and good disease prevention practices can go a long way toward maintaining your bettas' health. Consider it repayment for all the joy that your fish have given to you.

part four

Beyond the Basics

chapter 9

Breeding
Your Bettas

Although the average hob-
byist is unlikely to make a
lot of money breeding bettas, there is much wisdom
and enjoyment to be gained
by partaking in this fascinating aspect of the hobby.
Breeding techniques vary
greatly from hobbyist to
hobbyist. There is really no

"perfect way" to breed a betta. Many methods have proved to work
well over the years, but there is always room for improvement and
new ideas as far as breeding experts are concerned.

Bettas breed in two different ways. Species such as the banded betta
(Betta taeniata) and the painted betta *(Betta picta)* are mouthbrooders.
Other bettas such as the Siamese fighting fish *(Betta splendens)* breed
with the aid of a bubble nest that is built exclusively by the male.

Mouthbrooders

In a mouthbrooder's native habitat, swift currents prevent the betta
from successfully building bubble nests. Instead, the male carries the

eggs in his mouth, where they are incubated until they hatch. A single spawning among these species can produce as many as 100 eggs.

During spawning, the female and male will embrace, and eggs will be deposited on the male's anal fin. Shortly after, the female will "scoop them up" and deposit them into her mate's waiting mouth. This cycle is then repeated until all of her eggs have been expelled. After spawning is complete, the female should be removed from the breeding tank and placed in isolation so that she can recuperate.

The bettas' eggs will remain in the male's mouth for about five days until they hatch. After the young fry

Remarkably, eggs of mouthbrooding fish actually hatch in the male's mouth (Betta pugnax).

have released themselves from their father's mouth, they are on their own and will not receive any further parental care. At this time, the male should be removed from the tank because he may be tempted to devour his own young.

Nest Builders

The second form of breeding involves the construction of a bubble nest. This type of breeding is common among *Betta splendens* and other species such as the peaceful betta *(Betta imbellis)*. The eggs of these nest builders are heavier than water and will sink because they do not contain any oil that can be used as a flotation device.

After the female has expelled all the eggs, the male catches them as they drift down through the water, spitting them into the bubble nest before they sink to the bottom. This amusing "catching and spitting" game will continue until all of the eggs are hatched.

A single spawning can produce as many as 300 eggs at one time that will hatch in about two days. The male betta should be removed from the tank after the hatching process is complete.

The remainder of this chapter will take a closer look at reproduction strategies and techniques among the bubble nest builders. These particular species are among the most popular of all the bettas and are easy to breed and obtain.

The Breeding Room

A small breeding operation is great if you just want to add a few more bettas to your collection, or possibly pass a few along to your friends and family. This type of situation would require only a single breeding tank and a few jars in which to store the male bettas. The jars can be placed on a standard aquarium stand, provided it has some extra shelves underneath.

If you want to breed large numbers of bettas, and perhaps develop new strains, you will need a lot more room in which to work. Of course, a spare bedroom would be ideal. However, if one is not available, you will have to split the tanks and jars between several different areas of the home, which is really not practical at all. The moral of the story is to make sure that you look before you leap. That way, you won't find yourself trying to hastily discard fish and equipment when your new breeding hobby begins to overrun your space limitations.

WHY SEPARATE TANKS ARE BEST

Bettas will often attempt to breed in a crowded environment, even in a bustling community tank filled with other species, such as guppies and platys. However, this is generally not a very good idea, because if the male betta decides that the other tankmates in his environment are a threat, he may do quite a bit of physical damage to the less aggressive fish's fins and body. Another reason why you do not want to breed your bettas in a community situation is that the eggs and newborn fry can be eaten by the betta's tankmates before he has a chance to save them.

Another thing to remember is that betta courtship and spawning can be very rough in some circumstances, and other fish may end up injured simply because they were in the wrong place at the wrong time. It is much better in the long run to provide your bettas with their own breeding tank to avoid such conflicts of interest and territorial disputes.

Engaged in a "threat" display, this male betta lets other tank-mates know that he wants his own space.

Selecting Breeding Stock

To start, you might want to consider breeding inexpensive bettas in order to get a solid understanding of the basics involved in setting up a spawning tank and introducing potential mating partners. Inexpensive bettas will save you a lot of money, and you won't be risking expensive fish on beginner mistakes. But don't limit yourself by purchasing only two bettas. If space allows, buy at least three males and three females. This gives you several pairs to work with at the same time.

If you intend to keep a large number of males for breeding purposes, space will quickly become a major consideration. It is not financially practical to keep each male and female in its own 10-gallon tank. Females can usually be grouped together in one aquarium if they are all about the same size and have sufficient hiding places.

As you have learned, two male bettas cannot be kept together without fighting, and should be kept separated in gallon jars with a simple hose and airstone inserted through the lid to provide gas exchange and circulation. These jars can be placed side by side on a shelf. A piece of dark construction paper or cardboard can be inserted between each jar so that the males will not be able to see each other. If small jars are used, it is vitally important to carry out daily water changes to keep their living quarters clean and free from ammonia buildup.

Individual jars will help to keep the prospective males calm and relaxed until it is time for spawning. If the bettas are allowed to see each other, they will constantly batter their bodies against the glass and become stressed while trying to defend their imaginary territories and boundaries.

If the female has battled with disease before spawning, she may not be able to produce strong eggs that will develop normally. Even though fry can be produced from such eggs, the youngsters will often be defective or deformed. It is important that your spawning females be in optimal health and disease free before they are used for breeding purposes.

Unaware that they are separated by a glass divider, these two male bettas face-off.

Setting Up a Breeding Tank
THE AQUARIUM

A 10-gallon aquarium is a good starting size for a breeding tank because it allows you to carefully keep track of the bubble nest, spawning rituals and fry. All parts of the breeding tank (glass, equipment, rocks and the like) should be carefully cleaned with warm water and completely sterilized in a salt solution to prevent any lingering bacteria or fungus from attacking the eggs and newborn fry. Another way to prepare the tank is to disinfect it with a mild potassium permanganate solution.

Plants in the breeding tank will provide shelter for the female, should she need a respite during courtship.

THE HOOD

A tight-fitting hood will ensure that your spawning bettas do not jump from the tank, and will prevent dirt and household chemicals from entering the water. A good hood will also protect the nest and eggs, and will keep heat loss at a minimum.

PLANTS

Betta spawning can become aggressive, so it is always wise to purchase several thick plants. The plants provide privacy, can be used in the construction of a bubble nest and offer shelter to the female if necessary. Hornwart *(Ceratophyllum demersum)* or cabomba *(Cabomba caroliniana)* will work nicely when placed along the rear glass.

DECORATIONS

Providing your female betta with rocks and plants to hide in will give both of your breeders an opportunity to get pleasantly acquainted before spawning. If there are no plants present in the breeding tank, the male betta many eventually kill his mate out of territorial instinct before any spawning can take place.

Substrate

It is best to leave the bottom of the tank bare except for a few large stones that can be placed strategically in the corner for the female's protection before, during and after courtship.

Water Conditions

For breeding purposes, the pH of the water in the spawning tank should be between 6.8 and 7. The water should also be slightly soft with a degree of hardness between 8 and 10. This level can usually be maintained by using a mixture of 50 percent tap water and 50 percent demineralized water. Another method of softening water is to filter it through peat moss before adding it to the breeding tank. Reverse osmosis units and ion exchangers work quite well too, but they can be very expensive if you have a large number of breeding tanks running at one time.

A temperature of 82° is standard for breeding bettas but should be watched closely. If the temperature rises above 85°, the betta's eggs may be severely damaged from the excess heat. Higher temperatures will also cause rapid egg development, which can produce weak or deformed fry.

The water in the breeding tank should be kept at a low level so that the newborn fry can easily reach the surface when their labyrinth organs begin to develop.

Filtration

A sponge filter is ideal for your betta's breeding tank. The sponge filter will not cause the excess current that is commonly produced by large power and undergravel filters. There should be no heavy turbulence in the tank from any air supply, because this can damage the bubble nest and make it quite difficult for the male to keep the eggs or fry in the nest. Water changes should be carefully carried out every other day using a small siphon that won't damage the bubble nest. If filtration is not used in a small tank, daily water changes will be necessary to keep the environment clean.

Conditioning Your Fish

There are many bettas that breed readily, but others seem to have a hard time adjusting to their new partners. There are several tricks that you can try to encourage your bettas to spawn. No method is completely foolproof, but over the years certain techniques have been proven reliable and accurate.

ARTIFICIAL STORMS AND WEATHER

Water changes are very important not only to the health of your betta but to the betta's success in spawning. In the wild, seasonal rains signal the start of nature's breeding system. Natural waters become softer as they are diluted with fresh rainwater, and the nitrogen level begins to drop.

You can duplicate this effect by frequent water changes (about 20 percent per day for breeding). Clean, demineralized water will help stimulate the bettas enter their seasonal spawningcycle.

An increase in barometric pressure will also condition your bettas for breeding. Many hobbyists have reported that their bettas are more willing to breed right before or during a rain or snowstorm. By following local weather conditions, you may be able to introduce pairs during the winter season if you happen to live in a climate that supports that type of weather.

If you live in a dry climate, a rainy season can be duplicated by showering the surface water in your tank with tiny drops of water. This can be accomplished by using an inexpensive watering can purchased at a garden shop. Another method is to pour water slowly through a colander or any other kitchen utensil that has small holes scattered throughout its surface.

In the wild, bettas do not live in an area that remains at the same temperature 24 hours per day. Try fluctuating the temperature of the breeding tank. Drop the temperature to around 73° at night, and then slowly raise the temperature back up to 80° during the day.

FEEDING

Another common change in the natural environment during breeding season is the sudden abundance of live foods. As massive rainstorms sweep over the normally stagnant waters, a large supply of live insects is dropped onto the water's surface.

Cleaned, live foods, such as brine shrimp and tubifex worms, can be offered to your potential spawners to condition and ready them for breeding. When feeding live or frozen foods, do not discontinue the use of your betta's standard flake foods that you provide on a daily basis. These manufactured foods provide most of the vitamins and minerals that the betta needs for good health. Many cultured live foods do not contain these necessary elements. Live foods should be fed only as an occasional treat, or used as a limited spawning aid.

COMPETITION

If you have a male that is reluctant to breed, you might try introducing a second male in a sealed jar, placing the rival male near the spawning tank. When the first betta realizes that there may be competition for his female, he may be inspired to breed.

GETTING TO KNOW YOU

Bettas can be conditioned to spawn by separating the male and the female with a glass partition while live food is fed to both parties. Frequent small feedings will help the pair to condition quickly. The sight of the female may also convince the male to begin the construction of a bubble nest.

An alternative method would be to place the female betta in a jar and allow her to float in the breeding tank. Often, a male will be become excited just because a female is present. The glass jar will protect her from aggression and harm until the nest is complete. One disadvantage of using a jar, is that the female may become too excited and drop her eggs before she is released.

Choose fish that you find appealing for breeding purposes. Your goal may be to produce vibrant color or long fins.

Selective Breeding

A new color or fin type is always just around the bend. But in order to obtain the desired results, you will need to breed your bettas selectively.

BASIC GENETICS

To prepare for selective breeding, you need to choose several bettas displaying characteristics that can be intensified to produce *solid strains* (a related family of bettas that display certain characteristics carried through inheritance factors in the genes). These beautiful characteristics may include long fins, unusual color patterns, or other traits that appeal to your idea of what a beautiful betta should look like.

It is also important to purchase a female of the same strain as the male you choose in order to strengthen the line and to save valuable time that can be better used in the pursuit of a new type of variation. The breeding process used to produce a pure strain of bettas is known as *inbreeding.* The first step in this process is to choose a male and female that display a number of similar characteristics that you find interesting. After the first brood is born and raised, select a healthy male and breed him back to his mother. In the next generation, take the best quality grandson and breed him back to his grandmother and so on for successive generations. This will help to seal the characteristics that you are looking for.

As new generations are born, keep an eye out for any males born with unique characteristics that might be developed into new lines. If the female from the first generation dies, select the healthiest daughter and continue the line from that point on. Inbreeding is more effective than line breeding, which involves the mating of half-brothers and sisters.

Introducing Bettas to the Breeding Tank

It is important to introduce the female betta to the breeding tank before bringing in the male. Allow her time to get used to her new surroundings, and then place her behind a tank partition or in a glass jar before you introduce the male. Some males are more aggressive than others, so it is very difficult to know an individual male's habits before he is bred for the first time. After the nest is built, the female can be released safely.

Note that if you use a divider, the male may build his nest so that it actually leans against the partition. If this occurs, moving the divider may seriously damage the nest. Netting the female to place her on the other side of the divider can cause undo stress and keep the spawning from being successful. If possible, move the female by coaxing her gently into a cup where she can then be lifted up and over the divider.

> **GOOD PLANTS FOR A BETTA SPAWNING TANK**
>
> 1. Hornwort (Ceratophyllum demersum), floating or anchored
>
> 2. Water sprite (Ceratopteris thalictroides), free floating
>
> 3. Water hyacinth (Eichhornia crassipes), free floating
>
> 4. Water lettuce (Pistia stratiotes), free floating
>
> 5. Crystalwort (Riccia fluitans), floating

Moreover, if you use a divider, the female may drop her
eggs before the nest is completed. This turn of events
is all part of the breeding game, and as you will learn
through your own experimentation, there are drawbacks to virtually every method known.

With a heavily planted spawning tank, you may be able
to introduce both partners at the same time. If the
female has enough well-covered "safety" areas to which
she can flee, the pair may be left in the spawning tank
to breed several times without any serious damage
being inflicted upon the female by her partner.

Rituals and Nest Building
THE MATING GAME

*A courting male
will twist his body
and flare his gills.*

Courtship among bettas is usually quite flamboyant on
the male's part. He will often spread his fins, flare his
gill covers and twist his body to impress his female

companion. This beauti-
ful display of body move-
ment and vibrant color
can last for several hours
at a time, and is fascinating to observe.

Female bettas do not
sdisplay color and
finnage as the males do,
but will often darken and
may show barring on
their body. They may
also have a *papilla* (white
egg spot) near their belly region. A female betta will
show interest in a male by wiggling her body slowly
back and forth.

After the male and female are placed together, a rough
courtship may begin. The male will use any means possible to bring the female up to the nest, including tearing her fins. When the female reaches the nest, she will
signal the male that she is ready to spawn by dipping
her head downward. At this time, both fish will again
flash very intense colors.

BUILDING THE NEST

If the nest-building task is not yet complete, a male betta will build a floating nest carefully constructed out of tiny air bubbles that are coated with mucus from his own mouth. Some individual males will also use various types of plant debris to help keep the bubbles together. It is in this nest that the eggs will be incubated.

Spawning Behavior

When mating begins, the male will wrap himself around the female and expel her eggs by squeezing her. The eggs will be deposited on his anal fin. When

A male betta keeps watch over his bubble nest.

the first spawning embrace is complete, the male will fertilize the eggs and begin to gather them up. The male will blow these scattered eggs back into the bubble nest as they fall. He will continue to do this until they are fully hatched.

Several spawning embraces may occur, with small amounts of eggs being released each time. At times, no eggs will be ex-pelled during the embrace, but the mating will usually continue until all the eggs are released successfully. This cycle can last for several hours.

AFTER SPAWNING

After spawning is complete, the female must be moved to another tank or the male will most likely kill her. She will also need time to recuperate from the spawning ritual. There is a good chance that the female's fins may be torn or ragged from the rough courtship. If she has been injured, add a small amount of antifungal medication to her water to increase her chances of fighting off disease. Placing the female in a tank with good

A gravid female waits to expel her eggs.

filtration and water quality will also help her to avoid contracting a fungus or other diseases.

The female should be allowed to remain on her own for at least one week before she is placed back into a community aquarium, or with other female bettas. Her physical condition after spawning will be somewhat weak, and she will not have the resources or energy to defend herself from other fish as she normally would. Keep a close eye on her during this recuperation period to make sure that she is recovering normally, and remains disease free.

Caring for the Eggs

For the next few days, the male will diligently guard his eggs and return to the nest any that fall out. He will also add more bubbles to the nest as he sees fit. Often he will build other nests and move the eggs around to his liking.

Your Contribution

The eggs in your breeding tank can be damaged by lack of oxygen, which will slow down their normal rate of cell division. However, it is not practical to have a large amount of aeration in the breeding tank, because the strong current will destroy the betta's nest. A good solution to this problem is to place a single airstone at the surface that is hooked up to a gang valve. Adjust the gang valve's knob so that the oxygen flowing to it is restricted, allowing the airstone to bubble only slightly. This will provide aeration to the tank without disturbing the nest. Recent research suggests that overly intense lighting can also damage many types of eggs, and you would be wise to minimize lighting in the breeding tank.

Caring for the Fry

The eggs will hatch in 24 to 48 hours, and the young will hang from the individual bubbles in the nest, with their tails down. For the 36 hours following birth, the fry will absorb their yolk sac. During this short period after birth, carefully watch for any signs of water fungus *(Saprolegnia),* which can attack any unfertilized eggs. If left unattended, this disease can quickly spread to the fry and the adult male who is taking care of them. To avoid this problem, carefully remove any eggs that are unfertilized or dead before the fungus has a chance to develop.

FEEDING THE FRY

Feeding Newborns

Betta fry are very small and should be fed with liquid foods. Make sure you change the water frequently to avoid fouling the tank. Infusoria cultures can be fed through an eyedropper. After a few weeks have passed, baby brine shrimp can be fed to the fry to help them grow larger.

Feeding Maturing Fry

As your fry grow, they will prefer a diet consisting of both meat and vegetable matter. A well-rounded diet should include vegetable flake, standard flake, live brine shrimp, dried shrimp meat and a limited amount of tubifex worms. Small offerings of boiled spinach or freshly chopped lettuce will be appreciated as well. If your aquarium contains live plants, the growing fry will periodically nibble on them too.

Small feedings should be carried out several times per day. Remove all food that has not been eaten over a period of five minutes. Remember that young bettas have very delicate mouths, so do not feed them any coarse foods that can tear their sensitive tissues. Betta fry have a long gut and generally eat small amounts at a time. This means that they will usually be hungry an hour or two after feeding time is over.

MOVING THE FRY

Shortly after birth, you will need to place the young bettas in their own container. The fry can be placed in a small tank of their own, which should be equipped with a simple sponge filter to control biological filtration. It is dangerous to place large power filters or other mechanical types of filtration in their grow-out tank, because the fry's small size leaves them vulnerable to being accidentally sucked into the uplift tubes. If you do use a single sponge filter, frequent water changes will be necessary to get rid of any suspended debris that would normally be removed though mechanical filtration.

One of the best methods to remove fry without damaging them physically is to carefully scoop them up with a plastic cup and then slowly add water from their new tank to the container until they have become acclimated to their new conditions. The use of a net to catch fry is never a good idea, because their delicate bodies can be severely damaged by the webbing.

After the fry have been removed to the grow-out tank, they can stay there until they are old enough to have their sexual gender determined. At about three months of age, the fry will begin to show their colors and finnage. Males will be more brightly colored and have longer fins than the females. At this time, the males must be separated from each other and from the females.

Females can be placed together, but each young male will need his own small tank or jug.

SEPARATING THE SEXES

The females can be placed together in a single aquarium, while the males are placed individually in 1-gallon jugs. Make sure that the jugs have adequate aeration and clean water conditions. Frequent water changes will be necessary to keep their health at its best. After the second move, the fry can remain in their respective tanks or large jars and can be raised to adulthood. After they are fully grown, they should be placed in regular aquariums.

chapter 10

Recommended
Reading and
Resources

One of the best ways to expand your knowledge as an aquarium keeper is to read as much as you can about your aquarium hobby so that you will continually stay informed on current issues and new ideas. Books from your local library are one of the greatest sources of free information that you can use to supplement your aquarium skills and knowledge.

Books

Axelrod, H. R. *Tropical Fish for Beginners*. Neptune, NJ: TFH Publications, 1980.

Axelrod, H. R. *Starting Your Tropical Aquarium*. Neptune, NJ: TFH Publications, 1986.

Bailey, M., and G. Sandford. *The Ultimate Aquarium: A Definitive Guide to Identifying and Keeping Freshwater and Marine Fishes*. New York: Anness Publishing, 1995.

Bailey, M. and G. Sandford. *The New Guide to Aquarium Fish*. New York: Anness Publishing, 1996.

Braemer, H., and I. Scheurmann. *Tropical Fish: A Complete Pet Owner's Manual.* Hauppauge, NY: Barron's Educational Series, Inc., 1982.

Cacutt, L. *Nature Facts: Fishes.* London: Grange Books, 1993.

Cleave, A. *Aquarium Fish: A Portrait of the Animal World.* New York: Smithmark Publishers, 1996.

Dawes, J. *Tropical Aquarium Fish.* New York: New Holland, 1996.

Geisler, R. *Aquarium Fish Diseases.* Neptune, NJ: TFH Publications, 1963.

Hickman, C., and L. Roberts. *Biology of Animals.* 6th ed. Iowa: Wm. C. Brown Publishers, 1994.

Jacobs, D. *Know Your Aquarium Plants.* Ontario: Hartz Mountain Pet Supplies, 1980.

Mills, D. *You and Your Aquarium: A Complete Guide to Collecting and Keeping Aquarium Fishes.* New York: Alfred A. Knopf, 1986.

Ostrow, M. *Bettas.* Neptune, NJ: TFH Publications, 1989.

Scheurmann, I. *Aquarium Fish Breeding.* Hauppauge, NY: Barron's Educational Series, Inc., 1990.

Schneider, E. *All About Aquariums.* Neptune, NJ: TFH Publications, 1966.

Schubert, G. *Cure and Recognize Aquarium Fish Diseases.* Neptune, NJ: TFH Publications, 1974.

Scott, P. *The Complete Aquarium.* New York: Alfred A. Knopf, 1991.

Skomal, G. *Setting Up a Freshwater Aquarium: An Owner's Guide to a Happy Healthy Pet.* New York: Howell Book House, 1997.

Zupanc, G. K. *Fish and Their Behaviors.* West Germany: Tetraverlag, 1982.

Magazines

Product information changes quickly as constantly advancing technology is put to use in the design of more efficient aquarium systems and equipment. New products appear on the market every month. To keep up with rapidly changing aquarium technology, beginning hobbyists can rely on magazines to supply new information at a glance.

The following list of magazines will give you an even firmer foundation in aquarium basics and help you start on new adventures of aquatic exploration. You will also find many articles and tidbits of information concerning bettas and their care in all of these publications.

Tropical Fish Hobbyist
One Neptune Plaza
Neptune City, NJ 07753
Phone (908) 988-8400

Practical Fishkeeping Magazine
c/o MOTORSPORT
RR1 Box 200 D
Jonesburg, MO 63351
Phone (314) 488-3113

Freshwater and Marine Aquarium
P.O. Box 487
Sierra Madre, CA 91024
Phone (818) 355-14670

Internet Links

There are many interesting betta Web sites on the Internet that can help you learn more about your new pet. The following five Web sites are home pages that I found to be packed full of good information for the beginner.

Bettas On The Web:
http://www.concentric.net/~worstell/BETTAS.html

Adam's Betta Page:
http://www.geocities.com/CollegePark/4307/betta.html

The Betta Barracks:
http://www.aristotle.net/~vampyre/

Dave's Betta Page:
http://www.starpoint.net

Siamese Cyber Aquarium:
http://www.fortunecity.com/marina/sanpedro/122/
main.html

Clubs and Organizations

Clubs and organizations are a great way to learn more about the techniques involved in proper betta care. One of the best betta groups around is the International Betta Congress (IBC), an organization dedicated to developing new strains of bettas. This group is set up to share information on improving betta health and welfare.

After joining this great organization, you will receive a bimonthly journal with articles on all aspects of betta care, including proper nutrition, general care, disease and treatment, breeding principles, basic genetics from the IBC's technical assistance library and special announcements. The IBC also provides helpful information on betta shows, mailing lists and pictures of new strains that are currently being developed.

For additional information on this organization, contact:

The International Betta Congress
923 Wadsworth St.
Syracuse, NY 13208